*To my Jenny (Mrs JB) and my family*

*'It's simple economics. Today it's oil, right? In ten or fifteen years, food. Plutonium. Maybe even sooner. Now, what do you think the people are gonna want us to do then?'*

From the film 'Three Days of the Condor', directed by Sydney Pollak (1975)

*Version 2.0 (Bugs & Fixes). A revision not a re-write. To all my loyal test pilots and critics.. thank you!*

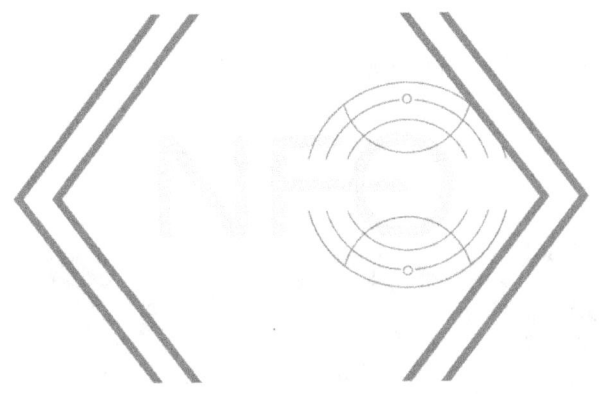

#newfundorder

***Contents - #NewFundOrder (v2.0)***

*Foreword by Tom Chatfield*
*Foreword by Robin Powell*

*Preface (p6) UPDATED*

*Chapter 1 - Travels of a Suitcase Fund Analyst (p8)*

*Chapter 2 - Optimum Economic Value (p18)*

*Chapter 3 - Fifty Ways to Skin a Manager (p24)*

*Chapter 4 - Oligopoly Orchestration (p32)*

*Chapter 5 - AM War Games (p44)*

*Chapter 6 - Key Man Misnomer (p65)*

*Chapter 7 - Supertanker Funds (p75)*

## Contents - A Digital Resurrection?

*Chapter 8 - Core-Satellite Conundrum (p111)*

*Chapter 9 - QED - Active versus Passive? (p122)*

*Chapter 10 - Clown Thinking (p149)*

*Chapter 11 - Chasing the Holy Grail (p168)*

*Chapter 12 - Digitalisation (p171)*

*Chapter 13 - Tesla Fund? (p186)*

*Chapter 14 - A Digital Death? (p198)*

*Chapter 15 - Revelations (p204)*

*Chapter 16 - Resurrection 2.0 (p209) NEW*

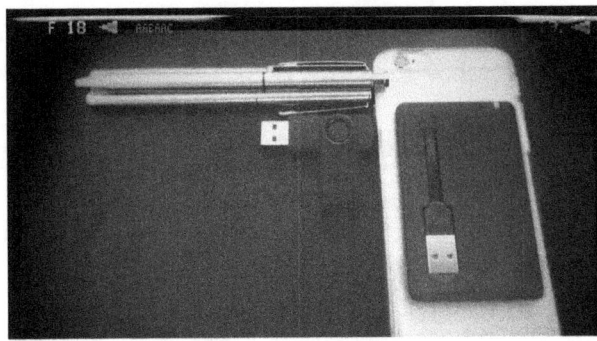

## FOREWORDS

We tend to over-estimate technological change in the short term, yet under-estimate it in the long term. In finance, we debate what machines will and will not be able to do - yet, as the book you're about to read sets out more clearly than most, we would be better off expending our efforts asking what we ourselves will still be able to do as funds become digital entities through and through.

You'll find blunt assessments in the following pages, not least the estimate that as many as 90 per cent of the UK's current 5,000 fund analysts may find themselves out of work by the end of the coming decade. What will survival look like? A willingness to challenge fundamental assumptions and hierarchies. An ambition as fierce as that of tech giants to look underneath the hood of existing industries, and to dismantle and re-tool every component as needed. And, perhaps above all, the appetite to join fundamental debates like the one JB sets out so frankly here: to argue, engage, dispute, and disagree - and to prepare for a tide of change that is already rising around our ankles, ripple by ripple.

BY TOM CHATFIELD, digital columnist, blogger, presenter, author 'Live This Book!'

It is increasingly clear that the active fund management industry, in its current form, is no longer fit for purpose. It's too expensive, too opaque and, in the vast majority of cases, it fails to deliver anything like the sustained outperformance that investors are paying for. There are many within the industry whom are happy to bury their heads in the sand. But as JB and other have repeatedly said, this is a crisis that won't go away until it's properly addressed. Those who embrace change will survive and prosper; those who don't will succumb to the inevitable pressures of market forces and go to the wall. My own view is that there are far too many actively managed funds and far too many middlemen; too many men in suits trying to get their hands on a slice of other people's investment returns. But ultimately the system depends on active fund managers, or at least genuine skilled ones, not least to set prices.

So, what will fund management look like ten years from now? How can we drive down costs, including exorbitant salaries and bonuses? Are huge super-tanker funds or smaller boutique funds the best way forward? And what role will there be in this new, improved fund industry for fund selectors? These and many other questions are tackled in this fascinating book. I commend it to you.

BY ROBIN POWELL, journalist and presenter of 'How to Win the Loser's Game'

## PREFACE (2.0 UPDATE)

Since first becoming a fund analyst, I have seen the number of dedicated fund analysts/multi-managers in the UK rocket from around 50 in 2000 to well over 5000 today. Following NFO1.0 many have questioned/refuted such a number but I have found that fund buyers co-exist in multiple channel dimensions, seemingly unaware of each other. The more I look, the more I find. Since the dot.com bubble burst, funds under management had grown (by 2015) over three-fold according to E&Y. The majority of global assets are moving into funds as investment banking contracts in the wake of post-2008 regulation. Casino banking has a new home: retirement savings. I am also reminded of my think-tank Long Finance's entertaining moc-doc 'Ultrahedge'. A spoof perspective of the rise of program trading, digitalisation, complexity and hedging strategies. You can find it on Youtube. Although I don't think the impact of digitalisation or demise of fund selectors will prove quite so dramatic; it is highly probable. I believe everyone has at least one book in them, some choose to share; others not, some either don't think about it or can't be bothered. Not all books are worthy of reading of course. In this book I try to anticipate the rise of digital and whether today's asset management has any realistic future in the new fund order (or not). I am subservient only to my own agenda. You can decide if that's of interest.

City or Wall Street, getting inside the head of a professional fund buyer is no easy thing. There is no archetype. Please indulge me to share some Brexit-free observations, as a fund selector, of the changes I have seen in our industry. I have never achieved the career heights of some of my peers, something I put down to a lack of early ambition to work in London. If that sounds bitter then I don't mean it to be. It has helped to mould me into something of an outsider, put distance between me and the noise of the City. I have stayed true to my profession even when knowing it was not the 'fast track'. I have always told my wife Jenny that I am playing the long game. In reality that plan may prove so long to come to fruition that the industry may not last long enough for it to payoff. In my time I have been a fund selector and strategist for well over a decade now. In that time I have worked for a medium-sized advisory, managing a watch list of funds and putting client portfolios together, I have been a fund analyst and product manager for a blue chip fund house, hired as a (tamed) fund selector, supporting cross-border fund strategy, fund development, requests for proposals, pulling together fund analytics and managing fund ratings. I have worked in group insight for a life insurer, mapping competitor activity, identifying key trends and reviewing business models, product governance for complex funds and investment products for a large bank wealth firm. Latterly I have been a gatekeeper for a large UK insurer, selecting new managers and due diligence of existing ones. Throughout I have remained at the front-line and have met and assessed over 1000 fund managers in my time. You can say I have been around. I have had the opportunity to see both sides of the table when it comes to asset management. It is in this context that I have reflected on what has been happening to the industry. This latest iteration is then a handy opportunity to de-bug any previous errors or omissions. #newfundorder

# CHAPTER 1 ▪ 'TRAVELS OF A SUITCASE FUND ANALYST'

*Inside the head of a fund gatekeeper*

Numbers. 15,000 miles, 40 managers, 40 pens, 10 moleskins, 12 days, 14 planes, 13 pairs of socks, 4 economists, 3 keynotes, 2 panel debates and 1 suitcase. I am no stranger to travelling but for a period in March and April 2014 I truly can say I lived out of a suitcase, a mix of obscene early starts, midnight returns, long and short haul flights, musical chair hotels and the life on the inside of an airport lounge. I know many friends who live that life year in year out, and while glamorous on paper it is far from jet-set in reality. If getting poor sleep, backache and bags under your eyes is your idea of fun then sign up to become a non-London based fund analyst. Of course there are some nice bits to travelling, you get to stay in some nice hotels, eat in some nice establishments, add loyalty points, but mostly I love nothing more than getting home, seeing Mrs JB, my cats, my classic Stingray car, my bed! Understand that I enjoy working in the buzz that is London; I love living in Scotland away from the noise. On a positive note, what comes from such travelling is a lot of time for in-flight reflection. 'Am I a good person, what is Jenny doing now, is there a better way to do this gig, do I add value, what needs doing next on the Stingray, when will my boss give me a break, what should my next tattoo look like, would I be any good at landscape gardening, will I ever be rich, capitalism, sociology, mortality?' The usual stuff (I have a busy mind). Inwardly I also pretend to be a secret agent or a contract wet work operative, when passing through airports, with my infamous indestructible black weapons-grade flight case in tow. My preferred wardrobe ensemble thus defaults to agent '47'. An arsenal of black coat, quality black shoes with extra heavy-duty soles installed, black leather gloves, white City shirt, red or black tie. I discretely play roulette with the airport security staff who give my case more than a second glance. 'Are you keeping tools in the case, sir?' They ask on occasion. 'Why yes,' opening to reveal my Glock, false passports, GPS tracker and a sat-phone (ftr, I do actually have a tracker in my case). I often wonder whether such a retort would inject some excitement into their otherwise mundane sheep herding but I don't suppose they would appreciate the bad humour. Of course I do not mean to trivialise something so serious but being a 70s boy I have failed terribly to outgrow my immature fascination for guns. I grew up with the heroic short stories Victor, Hotspur and Commando. Whilst lacking any true practical skills, like my father I love machines. I am also incentivised to behave by the armed police whom if I am not mistaken are sporting H&K MP5s. I am now through security (perhaps next time) but the thought enough gets me through the repetitiveness of airport procedure.

What is a fund analyst? Not a secret agent alas. This is the most common question I've heard over the years. By the time you can explain; the instigator has long lost interest. Years ago when you filled out application forms you usually only had the choice of 'bank manager', 'underwriter' or 'fund raiser' as a profession. Underwriter is probably closest. A fund analyst unsurprisingly analyses mutual funds and fund managers. A fund selector takes analysis and backs winners and fires losers. He 'underwrites' that a fund manager will deliver. My formidable colleague Bill Bulloch (formerly a hedge fund manager for Abbey National and latterly fund of fund manager at Cornelian) often talks about 'horses and jockeys', 'runners and riders'. The concept of winning is investing in a fund manager that does what he or she says on the tin. What fund selection actually entails is a strange mix of people management, intelligence gathering, espionage and investment research. It's not a vocation but given how long I (and others) have been doing this gig it ought to be.

Therein the fund selector pond in London is, in some ways, a perversion of the field. Perhaps it's due to the smelt in the summertime, enduring Tube heat or that visible wealth skew in EC2 or Mayfair. Perhaps. Fund selectors do a lot of walking, constant scurrying between meetings, a strong deodorant is a must to combat the musk. A few close quarter trips on the Tube are enough to know it's a losing battle. When I started out as a fund selector there was very little trade press and I could name just about all the dedicated fund selectors in the country. Originally funds were simply bought either by the adviser or sold by a pension company. However, as assets in mutual funds have rocketed, so too has the industry of fund promotion, distribution, media and selection. There are now literally thousands of fund selectors in the UK. Today being in the fund management industry in the City (either as fund promoter or selector) is an odd mix of conferences, fund workshops, media work, countless fund meetings, curries in Brick Lane, coffees around Bank and the odd after-event pilgrimage to Little Italy. Black ties and stilettos. What has changed in recent years is the ramping up of anti-bribery rules and the reduction in the volume and exuberance of corporate hospitality in fund management. Inducement is a dirty word in our industry. Events are becoming more modest, sporting events disappearing and single fund manager events being far more work focused. To be clear where I stand on this, I value good relationship management but I have never been swayed on a fund decision by the hospitality of the manager. However, I recognise that it could happen, particularly among wealth managers, distributors and advisers. If the new rules encourage a certain portion of the fund buyer fraternity to exit then I am all for. I will look back at the 'good times', but it's not why I became a fund selector.

The rise of the fund management industry is no more typified than by the lavish spectacle that is Lawrence Gosling's Investment Week Fund Manager of the Year Awards, now passed its 20th year. This black tie extravaganza at the Royal Albert Hall represents the glitz and glamour of the fund industry. For the first time I have been kindly invited onto what we (fund selectors) call the

'Jedi council' of fund judges. Likewise I have been invited to speak at the Fund Forum events in Hong Kong and Monaco, seen as go-to events for those on the distribution side of the industry. I am now asked to literally speak and attend events around the world and I enjoy globe-trotting. I may even feel at times that I have finally 'made it', but in truth I haven't. I may have been accepted to some degree but I remain largely an oddity of our industry, a 'turbulent priest' as one colleague coined it, a curiosity.

My own profile in the industry was largely covert until I began working with my new colleague, a known fund of fund manager in London. Until that point I had been working in what Bill today calls the 'puddle' that is Edinburgh fund selection. Subsequently appearing on the front cover of Citywire's Wealth Manager, in 2013, in front of the iron doors of St Mary's changed all that. With shirt sleeves rolled up, to reveal my tattoos, I certainly grabbed attention and for a day I wasn't totally confident if I would be grabbing my P45. Probability-wise I doubt CWM have had or will ever have a more controversial front cover, one that reached the very top of my organisation and not in a good way. Safe to say our press office was far from pleased and my thanks to JP (James Phillipps) for having the balls to run with it. It certainly helped our 'odd couple' demeanour and to kick-start a growing media profile. In that role I was Walter Matthau, he was most definitely Jack Lemon. Suddenly we were awash with offers to write articles and present. I was personally saddened when he decided to leave for pastures new, I do miss our arguments. However it has allowed me to develop my own persona, my way.

As with the many things I witter and twitter (tweet) about, I often draw inspiration from things I read from in-flight magazines upon one of 'the world's favourite airlines'. The name of this book follows on from my New Fund Order blog of the last few years. Having been writing articles, textbooks and short papers for some time, I wanted to go one better and publish my very own book. The biggest problem for books of this type is that they are, well, er, boring. They are written with all the dynamism of a party political broadcast. By contrast some writers over-compensate with pseudo-witty anecdotes. I did contemplate (momentarily) calling the book something more catchy like the Fund Selector's Guide to the Galaxy but (a) thought this metaphor a bridge too far and (b) conveys a level of wit within that can only disappoint the reader. Instead I have tried to relay a bit about me as I frequently use left-field experiences to discuss industry issues. I simply find it easier talking from what I know to explain things I know less about. My reasoning for the book itself is sound enough, to bring together different fund-related issues to try and identify a bigger picture. It is not a guide to fund selection, which is a far more difficult thing to capture, in truth I just like starting a debate, an argument, or a skrimash in Scottish parlance, which I get from my father and my grandfather.

For those whom have had the 'joy' of working with me, on

occasion I appear to do a good job of not listening to colleagues. A nightmare to manage, wilful, impulsive contrarian and creative. Obstinacy is not one of my better traits and I do try to subscribe to the theory of debate, so long as I start and finish it. Appearances can be deceiving and I have taken great guidance from those who I have worked with over the years; financial adviser Tom Munro, investment specialist Chris Arnott, ex-Templeton product manager and now Edinburgh University lecturer Stephen Porter, digital guru Mahyad Gilani, Honorary Professor of Glasgow Business School Alan Thornburrow, rocket scientist and leader of the Z/Yen think-tank Dr Michael Mainelli, journalist and researcher Jesus Soboral, Roland Meerdter of the APFI, market strategist Shiv Taneja, investment risk specialist Anand Sinha, Standard Life's Dr Brian Fleming, complexity guru Dr John Marke, insight analyst Michael Reid, corporate treasurer Carmel McLean, Hermes' Andrew Parry, colleagues including Bill Bulloch, Stuart Alexander and Scott Hardie. Lastly Ezekiel Cheever, a man of discretion and distinction, an artisan and a Machiavellian. I have benefited from their vast experience and thank the various industry publication editors whom have raised my profile and provided me a soap box over the last few years. I want to thank Nicholas Taleb for his book The Black Swan, which opened my eyes and Robin Powell and SensibleInvesting.tv, who opened my ears. I have also learned much about the workings of the industry from my network of fund contacts, to whom I am grateful, some I consider friends. My time in different roles has shaped me: curious, humorous, empirical and artistic. The entrepreneurial rebel without a cause, the perennial cottage industry peddler even when resident in a large behemoth company. My wife is a great inspiration to me, she is a far better listener, reader and team player than I could ever be, she is my greatest critic and support, Jenny has always kept me grounded in over 20 years together. She says I am 'special', which I think is a compliment.

I am not well read generally but I have read various books from within the fund industry, the most well-known being John Bogle's Common Sense on Mutual Funds, first published over a decade ago, and John Chatfield-Roberts' Fundology: The Secrets of Successful Fund Investing from 2006. The former is effectively the vanguard gospel according to the church of passive investing; it is the grimoire for active investors. It actually is a 'sensible' if uninspiring read. The latter book is more of an advertorial for multi-manager funds and represents sensible, if conventional, thinking viz funds of funds from the last decade or two. There may be books I've missed, but none of the books I have read have properly tackled the tougher unseen issues in our industry, from the fund selector's perspective. Often I think fund sales contacts know us selectors well, at times not at all. It is hard to tell when there is so much vacuous, superficial bullsh*t in our industry. To help, I recommend this book as reading for fellow fund selectors, fund strategists, fund sales directors, fund ratings agencies and fund development managers. This book is not intended to be a critique of different fund selection approaches, wherein I find very little evidence of the perfect formula. Fund selection will continue to evolve, or die, and for me it is about people management not numbers. Since reading The Black Swan, I no longer believe in holy grail quantitative techniques. Quant can only ask questions; not provide meaningful answers. If it could then any quant analyst is an algorithm away from being replaced by software. Instead I have looked beyond the immediate role into issues that will impact us all. In doing so I convey my empathy for my fellow fund selectors; and so that the industry may understand me a little better, whether that is of consequence or not. I am the guy sitting alone at the black tie dinner, standing apart at the fund conference, the outsider looking in (and out).

Take the time to watch SensibleInvesting.tv and it is clear we are undergoing something of a paradigmatic shift in the mutual fund industry. Observers like Strategic Insight indicate funds under management (FUM) forecasts have literally rocketed in recent years; with asset disintermediation away from banks and pensions, into mutual funds. Yet investor trust remains historically low. We have seen disruption from fee compression, passive providers and changes to the value chain from #digitalisation. My background with digitalisation is relatively modest. I have never worked for a digital start-up, nor worked and drank Americanos around the silicon hub that is Old Street (albeit I have read various articles about those that do). The closest I have come to Old Street is walking from the Tube around the big roundabout on my way to a stay-over at the Thistle Barbican. Instead my limited knowledge extends to working for an insurer in 2009-2010 where I briefly mapped the digital space for the end customer, monitoring competitor developments, the occasional chance to confer with more knowledgeable writers like Tom Chatfield and the odd seminar. My preferred office is mobile, on my iPad (many a fund manager will recognise the tap-tap-tap sound) but more often it's a laptop, sat in my employer's infrastructure-heavy HQ, with the odd bit of travel thrown in. My affinity to digital is therefore more aspirational than actual. Moreover the fund industry is wrestling with digital but so too are a number of other forces. The industry has been moving from traditional building block to multi-asset funds. The asset and wealth sector is amid a land grab of merger and acquisition, while platform wars rage on. Insurance companies face constraints from Solvency II capital controls coupled with the effective opening of the annuity market through 'pension freedoms'. Regulation is ever present and increasingly thematic; investor activist groups (like ShareAction or the True and Fair campaign) are more challenging. Investors now have far more routes to invest their money and engage media, creating new behavioural phenomena. Fund buyers are also reviewing past asset concentrations, super-tanker funds and mega fund groups, including value for money and the much misunderstood active share. The old script of Big is Best has been left in tatters. Investors are looking for new ways of investing, finding unique alpha, nimble approaches and hidden gems. The question is whether there is place for us?

## CHAPTER 2 ▪ OPTIMUM ECONOMIC VALUE?

*Optimum and Maximum Alignment of the Value Chain?*

It is March 2015, I am on my way to Hong Kong to present to fund delegates about my experiences as a 'European fund selector'. I am not entirely sure if I will make it as I have just been stuck in one of Heathrow's T5 elevators for 45 minutes, with a dozen other people including two kids and one claustrophobia sufferer. When the doors are finally pried open, the scene resembles 'Tenko'. So starts the beginning of a 50 hour round trip to Hong Kong and back. The flight over in business class at least allows me the time to mull on the topic assigned. Alignment.

Alignment? To begin, there are two ways I'd like you to think about how we align ourselves within the fund industry. The first is optimum. Think about a simple piece of string: does that string represent the shortest, straightest route between investor and the right outcome? The second is maximum. Take a Formula 1 race, with many cars moving in the same direction but everyone competing to win. Competition is normally held to drive good investor outcomes (in absence of collusion).

Think then of the fund value chain from investor to investment. Between the investor and their investment they may have an advisor, a distribution, a platform provider, a fund manager and a fund management firm. Each part takes their fee for the services they provide. Can we say that all parts of the value chain are aligned to the investor? For argument's sake, let's agree for a moment that there are broadly eight ways to create more alignment in the fund selection industry, from which both intended and unintended consequences can arise. They are:

1. Harmonisation, to establish common interests and goals from investor, fund selector, fund manager, distributor and regulator. This has been the utopian goal of the last 30 years but ignored misalignment and conflicts of interest arising from fees in the value chain. In truth this model has been breaking down since well before the financial crisis, leading to falling trust, falling fee tolerance and rising regulation. It is possible to build harmonisation through fund managers self-investing into their own funds. The ratio of that investment to total wealth tends to rise among managers of smaller funds and boutique owner-managers. However, investment and advisory trade bodies have failed to effectively engage investors, a task left incumbent upon intermediaries and distributors to bridge. This model is failing in Europe.

2. Optimisation, getting optimum economic value ('OEV') from asset to investor with the minimum drag of costs. This presents challenges for advisers in whether to add value through the investment, predict suitability, the advice process and or tax and family planning. Contemporary research indicates brokers have made poor fund selectors historically. The challenge then to active managers is the

growing support for the 'negative sum game' argument, that passive funds are a superior choice once fees are considered. This has been driven by a wave of academic studies, growing short-termism of investors and rise of consumer groups.

3. Institutionalisation, more of the value chain serviced under one roof. Alignment occurs through bundling different parts of the value chain into one product: wealth management, one-stop multi-asset solutions with a low advice front process. This gives the customer a single point of focus to compare service and outcomes. It is driving advisers to competing with discretionary fund managers, to compete with distributors. For example the growth of 'default' fund culture in UK and rise of wealth manager advisory risk-rated solutions.

4. Consolidation, the contraction of the industry to weed out weaker propositions. This tends to drive falling competition, market leavers, rising merger and acquisition. Recent Lipper data indicates that the fund universe is contracting and it has been globally since the financial crisis. Think about those recent M&A deals; in my 'Oligopoly orchestration' paper I noted a gradual move to a scale model from a margin model that will put pressure on smaller firms. A Harrington Cooper study questioned wealth managers in the use of boutiques over tried and tested core managers. The study indicated that buying intentions among wealth managers, into boutiques, was strong and passive buying intentions low, yet this jars with

the industry sales numbers. In my paper 'Core satellite conundrum' I speculate that the core-satellite model leads to an 80:20 division of assets and flows.

5. Regulation, which is all about conformity and setting a broad brush approach to alignment and the dictation of business models. The Retail Distribution Review is in full effect in the UK, the end game is the end of legacy trail commission, what we call in the UK the 'sunset' rules. Moreover MIFID II will see a number of changes that will impact fund managers, distributors and wealth managers. Anti-bribery rules are also reshaping the relationship between fund manager and fund buyer and we have seen the rise of Independent Governance committees and customer advisory boards, providing independent challenge to investment outcomes and value for money. If you are using UCITS then you really should keep track of the ESMA consultation page.

6. Compression, alignment by reducing fee drag on returns. Based on new business this by far has become the dominant alignment model in the US and Europe. It is the drive for fee transparency and fee pressure. The CASS paper on symmetrical performance fees is a watershed moment. Passive funds have been the net winners of this trend and net flow trends are now dominating new fund flows in both Europe and the US. In my paper 'Coefficients of inefficiency', I concluded that the total bill of large active manager teams has to come down to compete. Meanwhile my paper 'Key man risk misnomer'

cast a critical eye on fund selectors whom become too attached to 'star' fund managers. Whatever your view, agree that the volume of investor discontent is rising.

7. Disruption, investors break and shorten the value chain themselves. In many ways this appears similar to institutionalisation (above) but not controlled by existing distributors. Instead the disrupters are investors, technology innovators and government sponsored schemes like pensioner bonds. This will broaden routes to market for investors and challenge market share in traditional segments. Examples include: Government sponsored investment schemes and auto-enrolment of employee earnings direct into pension schemes.

8. Digitalisation, the rise in technology and robo-advice and its impact on the value chain is unavoidable. We have entered the age of BIG DATA and one thing big data does is it collates and removes traditional information advantages and creates new data advantages. Ask, what part of the value chain cannot now be digitalised? Google 'robo-advice' and look at innovators like AdviceOS, Invest-RFP, SharingAlpha, Finametrica, NESA, Google Money, Nutmeg and PureGroup. Digital does not respect geographic borders. Barriers to entry are coming down with increased cross-border passporting.

The common theme here is my optimum economic value ('OEV') test. Not all 'alignment' has been good for investors and not all future alignment is good for practitioners. What we are seeing in Europe is creating new fund management models and breaking old ones. Do key investor behavioural differences exist globally or is it simply a matter of time before all clients align? The rest of this book tackles some of these issues in more detail and forewarn fund buyers of changes ahead as well as the existing trappings of the industry.

*#oev*

*Pic. Hong Kong, Admiralty*

## CHAPTER 3 ■ FIFTY WAYS TO SKIN A MANAGER?

*Lessons from Madoff* ■ *Wet Work for the Gatekeeper*

Being a cleaner. Much of my role in recent years has been a fund governance one. Fund houses generally dread me darkening their doorways as there is a 80% probability I am there to clean up a legacy 'issue' rather than listen to the house's latest and brightest. The concept of winning in the City is based around tickets, lead generation, 'subs', 'reds', asset growth, sales flows to target and making 'bonus'. Back in Edinburgh I used to have a wall in the office; to it I attached news clippings and articles of the latest fraud, ponzi, inside dealer, pre-trade fines, client money rule breaches and boiler room. I would scour Monday's FTfm for the latest shammings. It reminded me and others that this industry treads at best a morale knife-edge and at worst is simply corrupt. With so much change afoot, it is all too easy to forget that not everyone in the value chain is sufficiently risk conscious or honest all of the time. Fund governance is a vital part of our wider corporate and ethical governance. We need fund governance but what kind? To recount a founding father of modern asset management JP Morgan, who said something like 'a man has two reasons for doing a thing, a good reason and the real reason.' I will add my own. We are only human, humans make mistakes, and some of us do bad things with people's money.

There is perhaps no one better example, of fraud in the fund industry, than Bernie Madoff. No better example of how professional fund buyers were suckered in. I want you to read a brief extract from Madoff's statement at his trial:

"For many years up until my arrest on December 11, 2008, I operated a Ponzi scheme ... As I engaged in my fraud, I knew what I was doing [was] wrong, indeed criminal. To the best of my recollection, my fraud began in the 1990s. At that time the country was in recession and this posed a problem for investments in the securities markets. Nevertheless, I had received investment commitments from certain institutional clients and understood that those clients, like all professional investors, expected to see their investments out-perform the market."
(United States v Bernard L. Madoff 09 CR 213 (DC))

Madoff's guilt was and is clear but there is also a complicity inferred upon the industry. Professional fund buyers had failed investors on two accounts. Firstly to encourage a culture of 'out-performance' and secondly to not have conducted sufficient due diligence (or at least try) to raise doubt about how Madoff's supposed 'split strike conversion strategy' was delivering returns. A fund buyer should only buy what they understand and that understanding has to go beyond the marketing brochure. Good fund governance should be at the core of fund selection. It is the most obvious way that fund selectors align themselves to the interests of their investors. Why? Simply that we have to recognise that other Madoff schemes will exist out there, other funds may be Ponzi schemes or that a background of difficult markets combined with a culture of out-performance pressures fund managers to take undue risk. Such activities do not exist in the Cloud; they are unrecorded, unseen.

Let's start by asking, what do we fear? It is human instinct to fear change. It can bring opportunity but also risk. We fear the risk of not meeting the needs of our clients. We fear not finding inflation beating growth and income, we fear staying alive for longer and funding ourselves in old age. We fear that regulation is making wealth management a zero sum game. EU regulation seems to fall from the heavens constantly and regulatory fees continue to rise. Fund managers and investors fear not finding enough returns in current markets, be that:

- *cash rates on the floor*
- *negative real yields*
- *high equity levels*
- *re-risking among mixed funds*
- *growing complexity of newcits funds*
- *gold in the wilderness*
- *oil getting fracked*

Collectively we fear the likes of Bernie Madoff and the reputational damage that those like him have havocked on the industry. He said he operated a 'split strike put' but instead we got split personality Ponzi scheme. For those familiar with Taleb's The Black Swan and his '1000 days of the turkey' story, I will leave you to ponder who was the turkey here. There were many. We also fear more Arch Cru's remain in the system, their cost to the industry, and the dangers of incorrectly assessing look-through fund risk. Arch Cru was such an example of incorrect assessment, both by the distributor and the fund buyer. Investors thought they were buying a cautious multi-asset fund; what they got was a fund with a variety of illiquid assets that quickly came under stress. Apart from being a good example of liquidity risk; Arch Cru also exposed the superficial relationship that can exist between distributor and fund buyer. Some time ago I read a subsequent Ombudsman Arch Cru case report, which firmly placed the burden of suitability on the shoulders of the adviser, yet the adviser had to rely on the distributor's fairly obtuse literature. Arch Cru tells us not to rely on past performance, volatility, sector classifications or indeed provider risk categories. Instead we have to take fund governance much more seriously, it is one of the main ways fund selectors can add optimum economic value (OEV) to their investors yet few devote much time to it. To 'lift the bonnet' and look underneath the literature.

I band the term 'gatekeeper' here loosely as many do, it's descriptive and to the point. I caveat myself because the quality and approach of gatekeepers can and do vary. So what can we do better as gatekeepers, fund selectors and scheme trustees? Well it's not spreadsheet governance (monitoring funds purely through performance statistics). Such approaches tend to be slow moving and committee-led. Contrary to what large companies think, committee bureaucracy adds very little governance but a whole heap of ass-covering in lieu of the next regulatory thematic review. Large distributors tend to default to aggregate monitoring and that pooling blunts how effective it can be. They also tend to concentrate assets in the same few large fund houses. The buyer may benefit from the well-developed risk management of larger fund houses, but it also means the consequences of risk are far greater if things do go wrong. By the time risk has been identified by the distributor it is normally already far too late for the investor.

What other fund governance options do we have? Well, we could devolve away the governance, but on evidence I would urge caution. We have seen a number of high-profile fund compliance breaches and a sharp rise in adviser-led propositions. Many of the large breaches occur within larger firms, a sense that risk teams are falling behind the onslaught of flows and trades. The biggest challenge facing adviser-led propositions, from an investor's point of view, is that they are usually created by advisory firms who have no experience of being Discretionary Fund Managers (DFMs). Without independent governance then I have tended to find conflicts of interest, inducements, variable expertise, insufficient challenge and opaque ownership structures. On occasion they can work very well but effective independent oversight has to be at the core of the proposition. We have to remember that the fund manager's first objective is shareholder return not investor return. Most fund managers are remunerated based on percentage of assets (not fund performance) and this makes the goal of asset accumulation all-consuming. At times there will be good alignment between performance and asset growth but so asset growth can also encourage risk-taking. Competition tends to drive under-performers to exit but it can also levy pressure on the fund manager to out-perform. Therefore delegating fund governance to the underlying fund manager is perilous.

Many distributors follow a mandated route rather than simply link to external funds. This appears an attractive solution to the problem of risk delegation. The problem is that the distributor assumes it (a) understands the asset better than the asset manager, (b) understands the customer needs better than the customer themselves or their adviser and (c) commingles ownership of bad outcomes. A mandate approach also has weaknesses. Often those monitoring the mandates are not experienced investment professionals, frequently just junior analysts or operations staff. Mandates also create a 'no flag - no foul' culture when in fact many risks could be building up within the confines of the mandate. Mandates are infrequently reviewed in line with market evolution and can lead to unexpected risks being hard-coded into the mandate. For example a minimum exposure ('floor') to an asset class that begins to display different risk (e.g. ABS funds through 07-08). Mandates can interfere with the fund manager's own risk management or be at odds with their investment approach and impact performance. Subsequent monitoring can become very myopic, analysts unable to see the 'wood from the trees'. I have seen other fund governance misgivings including:

- *Zombie portfolios where the caretaker manager does little bar the simplest of rebalancing*
- *The move of sub-advised funds in-house even when capability is in doubt*
- *An increase in manager changes, cost cutting, soft launches and weak capacity controls among others. These distort performance observations*
- *High-charging pseudo-tracker funds*

Many of these issues are the result indirectly from regulation, our own star manager culture and the wider consolidation in our industry. The problem is that there is no common approach to address these issues. Fund selectors remain a fairly disparate bunch, to be honest, driven more often by conventions than standards. We are seeing green shoots springing up through bodies like the New City Initiative, Association of Professional Fund Investors and the Chartered Institute for Securities and Investments. The industry has been firmly put on point by investor action groups like the Transparency Task Force, ShareAction, SensibleInvesting.tv and the True and Fair campaign.

I pose that fund governance remains somewhat behind the

curve for the New Fund Order. As things stand there are clearly good reasons for fund governance. As an industry we have a less than clear choice ahead: (a) to become more holistic and forensic in our fund monitoring and selection or (b) move to simpler, more controllable environments that reduce the need for fund governance. The former is supported by the rise of complex strategies and multi-asset; the latter by the rise of passive investing. Both could pave the way for industry-wide market standards. Only by putting our 'house' in order can we better align ourselves to investors and properly consider more enlightened issues such as ethical and sustainable investing. To consider, the following chapters cover some of the wider barriers. The fear of when things go wrong has driven certain investor behaviours: asset concentration, game theory and the rise of uncertainty. The superficial relationship and marketing machine of fund management houses, exposed by Madoff and Arch Cru, continues and is driving some peculiar industry phenomena. Have we learned? I mull over Madoff and Arch Cru as I head from my hotel in Commercial Street back towards E1 then EC2 for my next fund manager meetings.

*#whatdowefear?*

*Pic. Graffiti near Commercial St, E1*

# CHAPTER 4 ▪ OLIGOPOLY ORCHESTRATION?

*Why fund fee reform is creating a  
Premier League of price-makers*

With the rising pressure of passive, one threat to active fund selection is the growing concentration of assets into a relatively small number of asset management houses. Arguably from a fund governance perspective, fewer targets should make monitoring easier. That said, it may also be banking risks for the future and has a negative bearing on competition. Investors may rightly question even the need for fund selectors at all. Let me quickly rewind here.

I was on the return flight from London City to Edinburgh. It was the night after the IMA awards at the Grosvenor House Hotel and so feeling slightly less than pin-sharp you might say (helped in no small way by only four hours sleep, a few too many cuba libres and dancing in Little Italy until the small hours). The flight home was then a welcome chance to reflect on what remains an amazing spectacle with over a hundred tables of the great, the good and the others. A feast for the eyes of small glitzy dresses, vertically-precarious high heels, variable bow ties and the sea of cummerbund-restraining waist lines. The wine flowed, the rabble giggled, the insidious schmoozed and the collective basked in its glorious achievements. The results were in; the business was bigger now than before the credit crunch; well done to everybody. Despite the doomsayer's predictith the endith of days (er, ith) for the fund management industry; the evidence based on the lavishness of the 2013 IMA event would indicate quite the opposite. In the fund world the 2008 crisis is now well parked into the history books and the feeling was one of 'never having it so good'.

As a precursor I have been wrangling with this notion for some time without necessarily drawing a firm conclusion. It has been frequently noted that the fund industry (particularly in the UK) has been concentrating sales flows and assets into a relatively small number of fund houses and managers since 2008. In terms of outright assets the UK fund industry is bigger than ever at £660bn (2016: now over £1 trn) and the total UK asset management industry is now over £4trn (2016: £5trn). However, there appears to be less to go around and the industry has definitely been following the 80:20 rule of late. Source: Investment Association asset management survey 2008 to 2016.

Concentration risk: The numbers showed that the big are indeed getting bigger and at an accelerated rate. Assets under management of the ten largest firms have grown by 200% in just over five years. More disturbing is that these ten groups now control over half of the fund market compared to only a third five years ago. At this rate of growth these groups will consume the whole fund market in less than three years. While we must hope that competitive forces will slow this trend, customers who value choice over simply price have much to be concerned about. If only the OFT was quite so on the ball! With more assets come greater economies of scale, the ability to pay for the most marketable managers, CapEx to acquire competitors and marketing machines to draw even more assets.

Kick-off: The metaphorical penny dropped whilst reading the November edition of the in-flight BABusiness Life magazine, which I also accidentally procured while disembarking (your honour). There was an article entitled 'Worth their weight in Goals' on pages 16-20. The article talked about the disparity between the football player earnings in the English premiership clubs with those in lower divisions. In writing I am also reminded of the book/ film Moneyball which also addressed issues of exuberant salaries in baseball, itself an industry dominated by 'star' culture. Particularly it was a table on page 19 that first caught my eye. Source: Sportingintelligence Global Sports Survey, reprinted in BA Business Life 11.2013

*The world's highest payers by club and sport as follows: Club/Sport/Avg weekly pay/Avg annual pay: Man City/ Football/ £100,764/ £5,239,750, LA Dodgers/ Baseball/ £93,380/ £4,855,783, Real Madrid/ Football/ £90,734/ £4,718,172, Barcelona/ Football, £90,201, £4,690,430, NY Yankees/ Baseball/ £89,407/ £4,649,188, AC Milan/ Football/ £81,752/ £4,251,111, LA Lakers/ Basketball/ £78,671/ £4,090,742, Chelsea/ Football/ £78,053/ £4,058,742, Bayern Munich/ Football/ £76,924/*

*£4,000,036, Inter Milan/ Football/ £76,923/ £4,000,000.*

By this point in the flight I am suddenly reading the BA article more intently, I have just agreed to mid-flight coffee and have selected the biscuits (I wouldn't normally but they are medicinal on this occasion). The article continues to cite statistics from the Mail on Sunday (source: PFA) that the average weekly wage in the Premiership is £22,353 per week, £4,059 on average for the Championship, £1,140 for League One and only £747 for League 2. A quick add up establishes that the Premiership wage on average is 5.5 times that of the Championship and about 30 times than League 2. Having managed to negate the typical in-flight coffee stain and crumb situation I was struck by a very pertinent question - with lowering margins but increasing scale; is the gap in potential earnings between large houses and the boutiques similarly skewed and is that gap likely to grow?

Yellow card: It is a well-known dirty secret that the UK fund industry has been one of the most lucrative fund markets for over 20 years. It has enjoyed the best of both worlds: the open competition of the US; allied to the higher fees of Europe. The concept of the 'value chain' has had less to do with value creation for the customer than value creation for the fund manager, middlemen and distributors. Star manager culture has helped support higher charges and advisers bought in hook, line and sinker. Why else do you think so many large American fund managers came to the UK? Funds of funds became very much the de rigueur for over a decade as their double-tap fee structures provided an incestuous fee sharing between fund managers. Then the dot-com bubble burst and the credit crunched and suddenly high fees looked exposed.

Many confuse funds under management (FUM) with profit; or shareholder assets; the reality is that FUM is an input cost for asset houses. An asset business can run multi-billion portfolios and still make a loss if its operating margin is wrong. There is a term used in the fund industry but rarely openly discussed, it's how much a fund manager can 'sweat' their assets; (basically how much they can charge). The implications of compressing fees are that large houses will be less able to sweat assets in future as margins fall. What are the sign, are the revenues of the larger houses going up or down? Schroder's reported £315m in net revenue in Q3 2013, up from £246m in Q3 2012. Excluding the addition of acquired Cazenove assets of £27.2bn, Schroder's assets over the same period went from £212bn to £229.5bn (made up of £12bn in investment returns and £5.5bn inflows)*. That works out as assets being 728 times greater than revenue (or £1372 earned per every £1m assets, or 14bps for Q3 2013) compared to only £1160 revenue (861x, 12bps) for every £1m assets for Q3 2012. It would seem that Schroders has already achieved some economies of scale (not withstanding earnings from Cazenove yet unrealised at the reporting date). However, it is also true that earnings will not yet fully reflect downward cost pressures from RDR. Generally speaking earnings appear to be going up but at a slower rate than funds under management. Looking at the earnings results of a few of the other IMA Premiership revealed similar stories. *Source; Schroder's Q3 2013 earnings update.

Now the UK market is going through the biggest reform since polarisation with the Retail Distribution Review (RDR) and rising scrutiny over fund fees. I suspect that if the government wasn't looking into such a long-term savings abyss then it would be quite happy to keep the status quo and keep the taxes coming through the square mile. It is early days but the biggest presumption made about RDR is that it will force fund managers to become price-takers as customers become price-makers. RDR was designed primarily to target adviser standards in the industry; the coincident platform thematic review to unbundle fees. Fee unbundling should give customers more transparency but not necessarily more choice since that also relies on competition and a healthy fund market with many providers.

Platforms and insurers are moving to 'clean share classes' in a bid to get ahead of the RDR. Large fund houses are responding by increasing their asset bases in order to lower operating break-even points and improve their economies of scale to offer lower charges. As advisers and platforms find it increasingly difficult to in-source the investment component then fund houses effectively become price-makers. Smaller fund houses have far less leverage with distributors and therefore become the new price-takers.

Facing the loss of trail commission, advisers will become incentivised differently when choosing funds; soft incentives afforded by larger houses but cost will become overriding. I am not suggesting outright price collusion is occurring but every fund manager tends to get down to the same baseline with certain services such as global custody, fund pricing, audit and transfer agency all having well defined costs. The only ways to mitigate these costs is through economies of scale.

*Fig. Sweat? Scale over margin; conversely this shift will create diseconomies for smaller firms. In absence of a parent or preferential distribution model then smaller firms will become price-takers, survive as niche providers, sell or exit.*

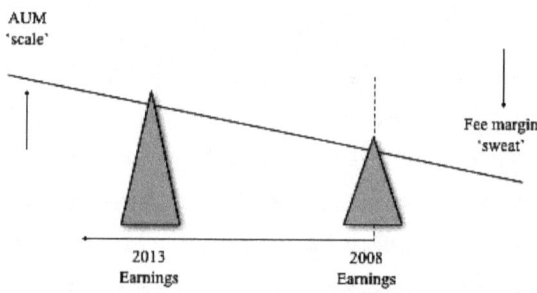

Although fund houses will be less able to sweat assets in future, (supernormal profits) earnings will continue to rise. Rising regulatory costs and increasing curbs on the ways fund houses derive earnings aside, fund houses can still become price-makers. The easiest route is by pricing-out smaller players from the market. Don't expect any intervention from the OFT or EU Commission either; without the benefit of goal line technology they will be too late. In short the large houses now need (and want) scale over margin.

Distributors are ostensibly complicit in creating these asset concentrations. They help support the launch and growth of retail share classes by linking to them. In turn fund managers have historically rebated part of the AMC back to the distributor. In most cases the 'rebate' should lead to a creation of additional units for the end investor, and therefore a lower net expense ratio, but the process itself is often shrouded. The benefit is unclear since the starting annual fund charge of a retail share class is often inflated and unjustifiably high. This process also distorts performance comparisons since the NAV is likely left unaffected. Here most distributors have been poor stewards and the use of fund rebates has been something of a dark art. There is also a question mark over whether all of the rebate finds its way back to the end investor. Distributor margins are something of a taboo subject and I struggle on a daily basis to get a straight answer. Distributors often bundle their own product fees atop of the fund charge. This makes fund comparisons even more difficult. The FCA's move to unbundling platform fees appeared to place life and pension companies out of scope (EU regulation may change this). This has allowed fee margins to go largely unchallenged and there are no common standards as to how fund rebates should be managed. They also distort competition for the wider fund market and create a conflict of interest for distributors. Whilst not quite the 1970s shady deals in smoky rooms, there is no clarity as to whether the end investor is getting the best deal (or not). Asset managers fear unbundling because it makes them price-takers, if everyone knows the bottom line of a fund then everyone wants that price. Rebate deals are therefore self-serving for both asset manager and distributor. What these deals do, however, is to confuse and conceal manager value for money. In just about any other industry such practices would be deemed anti-competitive and are hugely exposed to bribery and corruption. Noting both the IA's recent consultation and ESMA's incoming MIFID 2 and PRIIPs, this is an area both regulators and trade bodies should reconsider. Full unbundling is needed.

With the number of new fund launches falling, then it does not take a rocket scientist to realise that this trend is driving asset concentrations. It has given rise to a number of mega-funds (M&G Optimal Income, GARS, Newton Real Return to name a few). The negative consequence of this 'land grab' is that it leaves fewer assets for the other firms to compete for and thus hurts competition. This is oligopoly orchestration on a £600bn scale; let alone consider the wider implications for the £4tn UK industry.

Investopedia.com defines Oligopoly as: 'A situation in which a particular market is controlled by a small group of firms'. We only need to look at other oligopolies such as the energy industry to know these rarely produce good customer outcomes. Darwinism. Fee compression may particularly hurt smaller firms. *Consider Group AUM/ Earnings @ 0.50%/ Avg earnings p/firm means: Top ten IMA groups: £349.7bn/ £1.75bn/ £175m per annum. Next ten IMA/ £202.6bn/ £1.01bn/ £101m per annum. Next ten IMA/ £96.6bn/ £480m/ £48m per annum. Bottom ten IMA/ £0.54bn/ £2.7m/ £270k per annum. Source: Investment Association September 2013*

It is worth noting that there is nothing normally distributed about the distribution of earnings for even those within the top ten: with the top five earning significantly more than the next five. The reality is that fee compression resulting from RDR could drive many of the smallest IMA firms out of business. The more fees are compressed the greater the effect. For example, for the ten smallest firms in September 2013 then a 0.5% AMC is unlikely to be sufficient to cover the fees of the fund manager or FSCS levy; let alone front-to-back offices needed to run a fund business without subsidy. Step-forth the asset-gatherers like Investec, SL Wealth and Schroder. The loss in new business pipeline for smaller firms has been largely masked by the steady bull market of the last few years. When the market does eventually rotate into a more bearish phase then we will be better able to assess the extent of the problem. In the meantime expect more acquisitions and buy-outs. The BA article also talked about how the majority of football players enjoyed relatively short lives compared to the top players. Again there is a tempting (if unnecessary) comparison to be made here between the top fund houses and the longevity of smaller firms. Perhaps a better analogy to draw between football and funds worlds is the money being paid for football TV rights and the money being paid for acquiring asset books. BSkyB bought rights for the Premiership, 116 games per season, for £2.3bn. Aberdeen bought SWIP for up to £650m, BT Sport bidded rights for 38 live games for £738m, Schroders acquires Cazenove for £424m, BBC Match of the Day won rights to Premiership highlights for £180m, Investec took over Williams de Broe for £230m. Source: Sportingintelligence Global Sports Survey, reprinted in BA Business Life 11.2013.

The amounts above are an indicator of just how much these companies value the rights to access new lucrative audiences. A common theme is the purchase of more lucrative private client books over the common variety low margin institutional assets. It all goes back to scale and margin.

Playing the (80:20) offside rule: Facing a falling earnings outlook it is no surprise that shareholders of smaller firms become more open to acquisition; larger houses all too happy to snap-up the clients and asset books. As they are comparably cash-rich then larger houses can afford to make sizeable offers; the prize is size, long-term earnings and reduced competition. Those smaller players who do survive will either enjoy a preferential distribution arrangement or robust reputation in a niche sector. The large fund houses have become M&A machines: look at Standard Life, Investec, Schroder and Aberdeen to name a few. As the distribution landscape changes then so will the stratagem of fund houses. Some fund houses will target online D2C; others upstream HNW and family offices. I used to be in cross-border fund strategy and appreciate just how tactical fund houses can be in order to win. Whereas the last decade was typified by innovation, accelerating product development and rising competition, this decade will more likely be typified by a digitalised veil of 'multi-asset solutions', income products, passive-offerings and asset-gathering. Fundamentally reduced competition can never be a good thing for the customer long-term. Alas, the odds of regulators thinking long-term are very long indeed.

Fund selectors have increasingly moved assets from the many fund managers to the few, creating burgeoning super-funds. Be in no doubt that what we do is Darwinist, deliberate and divisive to long-term competition of the fund market and long-term returns of our investors. Free competition not regulation is the best friend of the investor. What is being sold as a champion of the customer will actually take away customer choice over the long-term. RDR has created a Premiership that benefits the few over the many. Making some cheap FIFA anti-bribery analogy is far too easy (so I won't). I've blown the whistle and raised a yellow card. Full Time.

*#oligopolyorchestration*

*pic. the target*

# CHAPTER 5 ■ AM WARS: COEFFICIENTS OF INEFFICIENCY?

*Big is not always best in the pursuit of domination*

It is mid-January in town. The City is still hungover from the post festive break and City airport has the usual 'driech' related delays (fog). I am weary from the fund drinks from the night before, which now in retrospect seemed awfully unnecessary with a day's packed meetings ahead. I sip yet another Americano and pop what I call the 'breakfast special'. Bright orange vitamin C tablet the size of a twenty pence piece, multi-vitamin tablet next, then paracetamol, ibuprofen, energy drink all washed down by a strong Columbian caffeine hit. A vein somewhere near my right temple twitches, then my eyes and then I'm good. For the next 2 hours I will be invincible, after then a gradual decline into the ordinary. Today is not too severe, the fog of the night-before begins to lift. There is no snow nor ice but outside it's dark, when it rains it is untypically Northern and familiar. I doth my city three quarter herringbone coat, black gloves and my Chicago grey Trilby to venture out, which is an ongoing source of fascination for fund contacts. 'Like Suggs from Ska..', 'You one of 'em Blues Brothers JB?' they chuckle. I am diplomatic and stretch to a half wry smile. 'No!' As I shuffle against the headwind between the palatial fortresses of one fund house to the next I am able to gauge the relative size of operations from the modest to the grandiose. There is an asset management war waging in the City and fund buyers are the prize. Glasses steam up then gradually clear. Fund reception, find voice, quickly recount my name and firm like the details of my dog tag to my enemy interrogator. Cough, 'Jon Beckett, from <insert employer here>'.

As assets have concentrated and the asset management industry barrels into this post-RDR paradigm - so are firms scaling up their research capability, product mix and acquiring assets. Can the large active houses continue to sustain the size of their head count as annual management charges (AMCs) fall to around 50-75bps (and below)? What sort of economies of scale come into play? Can the demise of ancient empires and contemporary defence spending teach us any lessons about the sustainability of such high investment stratagem? Where broker-led research is also set to reform, which houses are set to benefit from their in-house research capability? Is growth in asset companies cyclical, secular or both? Have historical active management fees skewed the active-passive management debate? Lastly are investors suitably recompensed for that intellectual professional capital?

'Size isn't everything' they say and yet fund selectors have long given preference to asset managers on grounds of 'strength in depth'. It is the reciprocal and riposte of 'star manager' culture but it has also helped support an ever concentration of asset flows into large houses over smaller boutiques. More people, more cost. Cost is a burning issue within the active-passive debate, one of trading cost (tangible and intangible portfolio management fees) versus residual return (active share and generation of alpha). Indeed it is the very trade-off of hiring in more 'skill' to expand research resources, against increased people and associated costs, that has skewed the active-passive debate thus far.

Let's look empirically at the head count and assets under management of some of the largest asset managers, and compares their aggregated performance. Fund selectors consider key, yet simple, due diligence questions:

> *1.     Is there an efficiency between manpower resources and aggregate performance?*
> *2.     Do acquisitions, super-tanker funds or passive arms impact efficiency?*
> *3.     Any correlation between overall fund fees and size of portfolio teams?*
> *4.     What is an optimally sized asset team for an active fund?*
> *5.     Does that number vary by asset class?*
> *6.     How many unique mandates is the team stretched across?*
> *7.     Does the current team contain staff arising from acquisition legacy?*
> *8.     Does the house operate an autonomous multi-boutique structure?*
> *9.     Is there a definable relationship between AUM and size of team?*
> *10.    When does too much in-house resource become inefficient?*

People Power? Growing up I was a massive fan of computer strategy games; indeed war strategy generally ala Sun Tzu or WW2 fascinated me growing up. It perhaps explains (partly at least) my obsession with industry 'war games' and plotting everything onto either macro, industry or investment maps.

Let's start with an obvious question. If adding people has a cost impact on the operational margin, then why do asset managers expand their portfolio management head count?

▪ *Add research breadth, and coverage of asset classes, to launch more fund variants into more sectors (country funds and absolute return funds are good recent examples).*

▪ *Better technical capacity to manage increasing book of assets ('more hands').*

▪ *Collecting specialists to help secure specialist mandates or bring sub-advisory assets in-house.*

▪ *Depose 'star managers' from other firms to lure legacy assets. OMAM's coup to attract Buxton or Artemis signing the Threadneedle US Equity team (led by Cormac Wheldon) are good examples.*

▪ *Enable technical advantage, depth of expertise, succession planning and allow cross-research between portfolio teams (e.g. multi-asset-cum-DGF funds).*

▪ *Foster reputation advantage and*

47

> *marketing collateral with buyers, ratings and media.*
> 
> ▪ *Gain information advantage in the price discovery and management of assets.*

Resources can be used in marketing to facilitate higher (differentiated) pricing. Sometimes head count expansion is a bid to protect or increase earnings revenue, sometimes in response to lagging or deteriorating performance. More often expanding resources are in response to cover increasing assets, while still maintaining credibility with fund selectors. Asset management firms have taken two divergent strategies to address relative under-performance and/or fund outflows. The first approach (seen frequently through 2008-09) was the cutting of operational bases, including reducing the head count of those costly portfolio teams. The second is to acquire asset books from other firms to increase the asset/people ratio and derive economies of scale from a flattening operational base. Certainly we observed some fire-sales through the credit crisis but more recently a number of fair-value to above fair-value acquisitions have occurred. The first approach is a product of McKinsey-like lean thinking (find me a firm not full of yellow, green, brown and black belts 'consultants' these days) but ostensibly a passive-defensive strategy. This approach tends to have quick but limited results; if the sector expands and competitors expand then the firm will lose market share. The second approach aims to capture market share. It is more costly short term but can provide a levy-like jump in expected earnings growth.

It is the more aggressive (riskier) approach as operational costs can become unruly during the acquisition period. The acquiring firm also had the difficulty of managing both the incumbent portfolio team and the inherited team from the acquired firm. The firm has to decide who to keep, who to handcuff from leaving, and who to 'release to the market'. I have seen examples in recent years whereby the acquirer has failed to pick the right line-up.

The first eschews leverage in favour of operational savings. It bets on competitors being unable to grow their asset bases sufficiently or being less operationally efficient. Such firms may have focused/preferential distribution streams and protected ownership. Fidelity, Invesco and Threadneedle are all good examples. Smaller houses often lack scale to acquire other houses and will therefore focus on growing assets organically and building strength in key sectors with relatively modest team sizes. Artemis and Hermes are good examples of this. In the face of downward cost pressures, more aggressive firms are leveraging their superior resources (people, systems) to manage larger scales of assets at a stable level of operating cost. What we have seen is a ramping-up of consolidation and acquisition among asset managers since the credit crunch and, in the UK in particular, in response to the Retail Distribution Review (RDR). Some firms have attained scale through passive propositions, which tend to be staff-lite by design. Examples include Schroder, BlackRock, BNY Mellon, Henderson and Aberdeen.

The role of the fund selector cannot be underestimated here. It is often the pressure (expectation) of institutional and large retail buyers that has encouraged this effective arms race between houses. Firms have responded to the regulatory and buyer backdrop by building assets and head count at a rate of knots. Most CIOs that I have spoken to lately all harbour ambitions to increase their asset base often through a handful of super-tanker funds.

The question then is whether our end clients have benefited from this expansion: whether more assets and more people mean better returns? The question is one of efficiency; the answer unclear.

Coefficients of Inefficiency: Parkinson's Roman Empire? The demise of the Roman Empire could be glibly attributed to over-expansion with a deteriorating support infrastructure and political in-fighting in Rome. It could also be put down more simply to a business that had grown too large, each component failing to add value over the next, a diminishing rate of return and arising vulnerability to competition (in this case barbarian hordes). Parkinson's Law ('work expands so as to fill the time available for its completion') could also be generalised as: the demand upon a resource expands to match the supply of the resource. Parkinson declared that after a certain amount of people were doing a thing, then the add value of what those people do diminishes. The world is awash with sayings but 'too many cooks spoil the broth' is probably most familiar if that 'soup' in this instance had an investment flavour. Parkinson defined a semi-humorous "coefficient of inefficiency". See Parkinson's Law: The Pursuit of Progress (London: John Murray, 1958). Anyone familiar with US defence budgets of the last 20 years, the 1970s British car industry, IBM in the 1990s, today's pension companies or Germany's Eastern front campaign versus Russia will draw easy analogies. I think this is relevant to the fund selector because I believe the asset management industry of the last decade makes for an equally good example.

US Defence Spending: Apex and Redirection? For years big Defence was best and great for business given the US is the largest armaments manufacturer and exporter in the world. To procure and twist a Detroit saying: 'weapons that blow things up on a Sunday, sell on the Monday'. The US has had the largest defence budget for so long that any changes to it rarely draw little attention from the media. Yet if you read the US Department of Defense's 2015 budget proposal (March 2014) then there has been a dramatic change in direction. The relevance of which will become clearer (I hope).

Triumphant 'liberator' post-WW2, yet confronted with a Cold War with the Soviet Union, and China, the US has worked hard to exert its military muscle within tight confines and to secure its resource needs. The last 50 years have witnessed a number of localised regional land wars punctuated by air and sea supremacy (Korea, Vietnam, Gulf1, Afghanistan, Gulf2) the US is left reeling with a huge national deficit, astronomical defence budget and precious few 'wins'. This sense of malcontent is only exacerbated by a national feeling for retribution post 9/11, a move away from Middle East oil dependency and the rise of cyber attacks, hacks, wiki leaks, intelligence debacles. The US is also facing up to its inability to solve new flare-ups in the Gulf or curb the territorial incursions by Russia and China. In response the US is scaling back and redirecting its resources to better meet the 21st challenges of fourth-generation warfare. The days of being the protector of the 'free world' and international policeman are ebbing away.

In early 2014, US Defense Secretary Chuck Hagel proposed plans to shrink the United States Army to its smallest force since before the WW2 build-up and eliminate an entire class of Air Force attack jets. The aim of the Pentagon budget was to aggressively push the military off the war footing adopted after the terror attacks of 2001. For example the Army, which took on the brunt of the fighting and the casualties in Afghanistan and Iraq, was already scheduled to drop to 490,000 troops from a post-9/11 peak of 570,000. Under Mr Hagel's proposals, the Army would drop over the coming years to between 440,000 and 450,000. That would be the smallest United States Army since 1940.

For years, the Pentagon argued that it needed a military large enough to fight two fronts simultaneously ▪ say, in Europe and Asia. More recently the military has been ordered to downsize that ambition. The subsequent budget announced did appear to follow Hagel's proposals, in which the DoD wrote: 'The Department achieves a balanced approach by reviewing all areas of the budget for potential savings. This includes achieving new efficiencies, eliminating duplication, reducing management headquarters and overhead, tightening personnel costs, enhancing contract competition, terminating or restructuring weapons programs and consolidating infrastructure.' What that means in practice is a move away from large-scale land war capability to a broader nimbler mandate, one with reducing manpower. The backdrop is cost pressure.

Defence is big business and the change in the DoD's direction may reverberate with some fund strategists. Asset firms have for years followed a fairly simple strategy of: acquire asset commitments, launch fund, seed fund, gather assets, seed and launch next fund and so on until the firm has a fund in every sector. Fund development was obsessed about gap-analysis and with 34 IMA sectors (plus offshore equivalents) then it is not uncommon for larger fund houses to have well in excess of 50 live funds. The problem then is that it is harder to close funds than launch and the industry is full of old outmoded legacy funds that still have investors and earn revenue but also, critically, require people to manage them. These funds absorb resources and can dilute a team's aggregated performance due to mandate limitations. If resources are pared back on old funds then performance tends to deteriorate. Firms now have a difficult choice: to stay big and try to capture market share through broad coverage, acquisition and large head count or to be more focused, nimbler with smaller head count. With the rise of super-tanker funds and multi-asset investing it is possible (if not necessarily desirable) to manage over £50bn with only a handful of mandates.

The first approach can lead to inefficiency and declining aggregate performance but may be offset by having sufficient top performing flagship funds and a large revenue base. Having broad coverage improves the chances of having winners (and losers). The second option reduces the likelihood of poor aggregate performance, by focusing resources, but the firm may lack sufficient headline funds in the right sectors, at the right time, and therefore a more volatile/concentrated revenue stream plus more concentrated redemption risk. That trend has already shown itself through slowing numbers of Pan-European fund launches and rising fund closures. The fund universe is gradually shrinking.

Research Warfare: Disarmament of 'Sell Side' Brokerage? One variable to consider can be found in changes to broker research and the way it is paid. Tough new rules are being introduced across Europe that may curb the use of broker research by active fund managers. This move may potentially hinder boutiques ability to compete with the global asset managers with large in-house research teams. 'Sell-side' research, as it is commonly referred, is a popular tool of the active manager, purchased to help the price discovery of an asset. The use (or not) of external research is a key factor in how an asset manager structures a portfolio team to cover x£m assets. Consequently, changes to relating rules may have a large bearing on how a firm conducts research, the competitive landscape between firms and strategic rationale for building a firm's in-house research capability. It is worth stressing again that these rules primarily impact active rather than passive asset managers.

In late 2013, the FCA issued consultation CP13/17 on the banning of dealing commission. An overriding consideration for the FCA is the protection of investors and the removal of unfair practices and costs therein. This should also include ensuring long-term competition in the fund industry, mitigating barriers to entry and not over-penalising smaller firms that rely on broker research versus larger fund houses that can leverage proprietary research and economies of scale with research providers. This threat to competition was already (indirectly) highlighted in the OFT's reports into workplace pensions in September 2013. I am in broad agreement with the points publicly stated by the IMA in its report 'The Use of Dealing Commission for the Purchase of Investment Research'. Specifically moving to an open and transparent basis is appropriate in terms of treating customers fairly. Problematically, a move to a 'cash model' may increase costs for smaller firms that are already facing diseconomies of scale, as the result of price unbundling following RDR and platform review. The IMA stressed in particular that creating a pure cash market for professionals into multi-asset teams. This follows the model developed by Standard Life Investments for the GARS multi-asset team.

Group-specific observations include:

BlackRock: Huge assets should drive economies of scale via an acquired passive business (from Barclays) and shrewd acquisitions (including once giant Merrill Lynch) through the credit crisis, nicely backed by Bank of America. However, that benefit has not necessarily translated into strong relative performance across its active funds. BlackRock easily has the most professionals overall (527) and those narrow margin passive assets will not support an under-performing active desk for long. In the UK, BlackRock has rested heavily on its UK Equity and Gold & General funds, which have come under pressure. BlackRock has focused some time on its passive business since buying from Barclays; more recently we have seen signs that BlackRock is also shifting investment within its active business in favour of the multi-asset proposition.

Newton: The multi-boutique approach of parent BNY Mellon means that Newton does not obviously benefit from economies of scale other than through BNY's distribution such as the US. The house suffers some redemption risk in terms of asset concentration around Real Return and Global Higher Income funds. As-is Newton still appears to have good scale across its Equity and Multi-asset funds married to decent performance but I expect CIO Simon Pryke to make some tough decisions over his fund offering, as he chases £50bn AUM.

Threadneedle: Assets appear well scaled across asset classes following a few years of strong performance and inflows into its 'select' equity funds and property offering. Threadneedle appears to now be enjoying some economies of scale with sister brand Columbia and those resources have not been factored in. The team of 118 is relatively well distributed across the asset classes. Unfortunately the loss of Cormac Wheldon's US Equity team is an unquestionable blow and follows the departure of global select manager Jeremy Podger in 2011. Parent Ameriprise now have to weigh how to focus the house and whether to introduce Columbia funds into the UK.

Artemis: Artemis' relatively small fund offering reflects its boutique-focused beginnings. Head count is scaled appropriately and better than the peer median. This is well illustrated by having only 21 equity professionals, only three more than Hermes while running around three times the Equity AUM. Artemis has longed to breakaway from its origins in managing UK long-only assets. Stealing Threadneedle's US equity team helps Artemis to push its global capability. This strategy seems prudent given the trend of flows in favour of global and multi-asset funds. Where Artemis will still need to invest is in its multi-asset offering with only five professionals currently quoted. It will also need to adapt from its volatile origins to a more stable performing proposition.

research could throw up obstacles for start-up investment managers by raising barriers to entry and could have unintended impacts on SME research. This creates the potential to disadvantage smaller resourced asset managers in favour of larger firms. This may seem at best a footnote but the expected development of this regulation may be a key variable in asset managers' strategic outlook for the next 3-5 years and resource planning for the foreseeable future. It also has a disproportionate impact on equity funds.

Asset Management Firms: AUMs and Head Counts? Getting to the point, how do asset management firms compare in terms of head count as a ratio of assets managed? How do these teams compare in terms of aggregate performance? (The all-essential bang for buck). The first obvious thing to jump is out is the huge skew created by BlackRock's equity assets. It is worth remembering that a large proportion of which is passively managed. Comparing median results of groups indicates that the best economies of scale occur for multi-asset funds. This should be unsurprising as these desks often leverage the cross analysis from the other desks but already gives some indication that these strategies can be subsidised by equity and bond funds. Despite the skew of the BlackRock results, Equity funds have the most concentrated assets per head count, a legacy that goes back to how industrial sectors are often covered by dedicated specialists and hence equity desks tend to have more analysts. In future I expect a migration of equity and bond

Fidelity FIL Ltd: Fidelity's overall figures are broadly in line with the peer median but skewed by better scale across bond and multi-asset teams and poorer scale in its equity offering. Fidelity has the second biggest equity team (227) in the sample group, a long-standing key sales point of Fidelity. Going forward, Fidelity continues to undergo change with a refocus of its multi-asset Investment Solutions Group following retirement of Richard Skelt and purchase of the GEOD passive provider in the US. A multi-asset team of only 23 will likely require further investment over the next few years. Fidelity has also lost UK market share in recent years and may find it challenging to retain and market that traditional 'research' advantage.

Schroders: Schroders has been the quintessential scale player for the last few years, culminating in a large investment in both fixed income and multi-asset teams and the acquisition of Cazenove. The fixed income team (141) can now rival any other, in terms of size, and shows a clear gambit to build assets, most likely as a support arm to the group's growing presence in the multi-asset market (91 professionals) and fixed income more generally AUM across bond-biased Europe. In the event that the multi-asset team retrench away from fixed income, or the firm fails to gather bond assets, then I would expect Schroders to cut back its fixed income team over the next five years. Lastly, with the greatest number of equity professionals (271) that legacy looks sub-optimal and I would expect further consolidation post-Cazenove as the business continues to leverage existing resources to support the multi-asset proposition.

UBS: UBS has ostensibly been in a phase of recovery and rebuild following the credit crisis and taboo Asian 'black-box' outflows. UBS has one of the largest legacy fund ranges (well over 700). With 192 professionals, UBS' equity offering has the poorest scale versus assets, in the sample group, and I would expect restructuring to be likely if no new AUM is forthcoming. Part of the issue may lie in the large number of legacy funds and restructuring and consolidation is a likely and prudent strategy. Performance across the fund range is best described as varied. By comparison the group's bond (145) and multi-asset (90) teams look better scaled relative to AUM (albeit the bond team has four more professionals than Schroders).

Hermes: Hermes enjoys a preferred distribution through its legacy as asset manager of the BT pension scheme. Since re-branding, Hermes has managed to attract over a dozen other large institutional clients. Hermes' relatively small AUM (smallest in the sample) perhaps dictates what first appears to be an odd distribution of resources. Most of its 35 quoted professionals (in 2013) were equity focused and only four in fixed income. Hermes' multi-asset offering remains *de minimis* and clearly an area the house needs to address, especially as institutional clients continue to migrate in that direction. Update: The recent launch of their dynamic multi-asset fund appears to be a step in the right direction and importantly the firm has a new style of leadership under the charismatic Saker Nusseibeh.

Henderson: Henderson's head count (168) is a legacy of acquisitions of New Star and Gartmore businesses. While Henderson does not have the largest portfolio team (104) outright, in proportion of people to assets it is the most concentrated. This is especially so for the 100+ equity team under Graham Kitchen and I expect more consolidation will be necessary should Henderson fail to attract significant assets. Overall Henderson is at risk of diseconomies of scale and people costs detracting from the potential value-add of the team. This will only come to bear in a falling AMC environment and something Henderson can offset through a number of strong performing funds. Henderson also lacks a large multi-asset team (14) and an obvious area for investment for the next few years.

Bang for Buck. Performance comparisons proved difficult due to high survivorship bias, sheer number of funds involved and diversity of product maps. Of the firms compared the general trend was one of better relative returns among smaller more compact propositions. This is unsurprising as larger propositions are more likely to have older legacy funds. More pertinent to the question of this chapter, was that there was no clear performance advantage among those houses with larger portfolio teams than those with more compact teams. Reasons for were inconclusive but some relationship between AUM and number of funds existed and a larger portfolio team may simply be a function of having to manage more funds. That creates a notion of subsidy, i.e. that the overall operating cost of a large team has to be burdened across all investors (new and old) whereas a boutique will not suffer the same dilemma even if it cannot benefit from quite the same operational economies of scale.

Decision Dichotomy? One obvious point not mentioned thus far is that more globally diverse asset firms have a higher propensity to want and arguably require professionals in a number of locations, industry sectors and asset classes. I am a supporter of active fund management, global research, depth of expertise, local specialist knowledge, the discovery of intrinsic value and opportunity. In many ways then I write this chapter not with glee but with sad resignation that many research teams will simply prove more difficult to sustain if not profitably backed with commensurate scale in assets.

Clearly aggregated performance is a blunt tool for comparison but does help to give some feel of how resources are focused, stretched and potentially diluted. As an asset firm, it is not in your interest to have weak performing funds on the proposition; yet survival of the weakest makes a sweeping assumption of the apathy among distributors and investors. Until now firms may have been able to extract attractive AMC for very little management resource (or alpha) but Active Share, RDR and changes to the annuity market in 2015 will test this.

Therefore asset management firms have a number of tough choices ahead, whether to focus on active or passive operations, to invest in multi-asset, which funds to launch (and close) and what resources are required for the next decade. There are more equity sectors in the IMA/ABI classifications that for any other asset class, a legacy of the 1990s-2000s building block popularity. Yet 80% of assets are being herded into only 20% of those sectors and therein 80% of assets are being attracted to only 20% of available funds. Competition in the fund universe has been far from healthy since the credit crisis and this fact is beginning to land home with asset management firms. Cost pressures look set to squeeze earnings and there is a growing divide in terms of net flows between winners and losers. This has left the equity desks among some fund houses swollen, compared to the assets/inflows into bond and multi-asset teams. If AMCs reduce then the portfolio cost per x£m of AUM managed becomes more progressively difficult to support.

Cost-cutting in some desks, to some extent, had been offset by rising salaries, generally, as traders migrated from investment banking to asset management. Casino banking has a new home; it is called your pension fund. As the market continues to move towards multi-asset solutions, over building blocks, then I expect to see the largest cost-cutting to occur within equity teams over the next five years. Firms need to begin to reconsider their strategies: whether to expand or to focus, to push building block or solutions, to be a scale player or to be nimble. People growth will likely come in expanding multi-asset capability and the redeployment of existing resources to support those solutions. Building block funds will continue to service the institutional market, particularly DFMs and asset allocators whom lack internal capability to run direct assets. That product mix will drive which funds to keep open and how many people are absolutely necessary to the running of those assets. This is a game-changer for asset management. War Games.

*#amwargames*

*Pic. Will the next AM War be a digital one?*

## CHAPTER 6 ▪ KEY MAN MISNOMER?

*Huss under a bus, spyfilm or liking the cut of one's jib?*

Coffees and chit chats. The City does most of its deals in bistros, restaurants and coffee houses. You need only frequent the Royal Exchange ('the RE') near Bank to validate this assertion. I've mentioned already that fund selection is a people management role. Maintaining a good fund relationship network is essential to keeping one step ahead of the adviser herd. Above all, fund selectors hate surprises and hate even more being the last to know. Think of it a bit like a spook and his 'asset'. Many a thing is said between fund manager and selector, within the 'confines of four walls', and between fund contacts in a coffee house. Take a bleak rainy February morning. A shadowy fund selector sat in the back corner of Neros, scanning the Monday edition of FTfm, sipping on a flat white, stern brow focused on the latest movings and shakings. In stepped his fund contact, for drama let's call him Giles Brunting-Brown ('BB' or 'Brunters') who had come in from the cold. BB's fund house had issued a press release, the big name was leaving for a rival crew and BB's face was one of fear. He knew the redemption bell was about to be rung. The fund selector got a tip-off call at 7am before the news broke. BB offered the fund selector another caffeine-enriched beverage, the gatekeeper accepted. It ticked the anti-bribery (FCA FG13/1) box. In truth the fund selector didn't care for the big name anyway, who he felt was still trading on the success of yesteryear but redemptions are another matter. 'Reds' as they are known are the bane of the fund management industry. Redemptions can force sells and hurt performance. Not only of the fund in question but often sister funds as well. Moves also change the dynamic of a team, sometimes good, sometimes bad. Today the fund selector wanted details, defender information and intel on the rest of the portfolio team. Any likelihood of further defections, planned 'lock-ins', any secondary impact from planned shuffles? They talked, some assurances were exchanged, the fund held but put 'on watch'. BB was thankful, trust maintained. A pro-caffeine fund selector may literally repeat such meetings hundreds of time a year. That's a lot of coffee.

In the UK fund industry, our obsession over team size pales into insignificance to our continued obsession for 'star' fund managers. Ironic that the two are connected. Time and time again I see it rear its head, the cynical popularity contest that is the distributor 'gap-fill' exercise. This is the common term distributors and fund houses term their product map, identifying gaps in perceived quality sector-by-sector. During the era of open architecture, it was a numbers game, all about how many funds per sector a platform could boast. Within guided architecture it was all about the median performance and chasing top quartile managers. Instead of adding potentially superior fund managers today; and those hidden gems, sales colleagues default to well-known fund managers. This is being driven by advisers (themselves not fund experts) and exploited mercilessly by the marketing machines of the big asset firms. It is the side of a black cab or that glossy ad in the pinks. At the core of this form of fund selection is personality, reputation, ratings and awards. These inputs are often circular, often based on perceived 'alpha' from previous years. Like a political election, the system is ostensibly full of spin and a big barrier to entry for smaller boutique firms.

Huss under a bus? It is probably the most common term used for key man risk (KMR) today and used for as long as I can remember, certainly since John Husselbee was at Henderson and for no reason I can think of other than it rhymed. Talking of the 'Huss', I always thought he would make a good spy film character, I think it's the glasses in recent years. The tenuous link being that when growing up I liked a good spy film, my favourites being 'Gorky Park' with William Hurt (1983) and 'Three Days of the Condor' with Robert Redford (1975). In one statement I have probably typified my age, gender and beliefs more than at any other time.

> *IMDB says Gorky Park is about 'An investigator on the Moscow police force relentlessly pursues the solution to a triple homicide which occurred in Moscow's Gorky Park. He finds that no one really wants him to solve the crime because it is just the tip of a complex conspiracy which involves the highest levels of the Moscow city government.' Directed by Michael Apted.*

> *IMDB says Three Days of the Condor is about 'A bookish CIA researcher finds all his co-workers dead, and must outwit those responsible until he figures out who he can really trust.' Directed by Sydney Pollak.*

What I and others liked about these films were the lead actors, their ingenuity in the face of adversity and in many ways we want our favourite managers to be a bit like those characters: intelligent, considered, experienced and stealthy. For well over a decade we fund selectors have become obsessed about fund managers, to characterise them, to invest on the strength of what they say, what they do, who they are. This obsession has been fueled by the mighty marketing machines of the fund houses and indeed publications like the one you are reading now; when managers leave, it then becomes the biggest news of the day and continues to divide fund selectors.

Darwinism is not Evolution. As fund selectors we have increasingly moved assets from the many fund managers to the few, creating burgeoning super-funds. Be in no doubts that what we do is Darwinist, deliberate and divisive to long-term competition of the fund market and long-term returns of our investors. Oligopolies are not considered good in economic terms and I feel the noise we have seen around the Woodford and Munro departures simply mask underlying concerns over the size their funds had grown to. Effectively some of the biggest fund selectors are getting on their perches to either defend their decision to feed assets in or justify why they are moving assets out. Be in no doubt there is a lot of professional ego being horse-traded over these departures.

We commonly talk in fund circles about 'Woodford' (referring to Neil Woodford), 'Buxton' (Richard Buxton) or 'Broughy' (Andy Brough). While a lucky few of us can boast being on first-name terms with these giants, I can assure you that they are far more memorable to us than we are ever to them. Meanwhile, our fund house account managers are keen to nurture our egos and it's a game we are all keen to play over the hallowed 'name drop over a pint' scenario. We like to refer to fund managers in personal terms when writing to investors and discussing among peers, we exert our esteem through our familiarity with fund managers. The sub-text is that we want to convey our information advantage; why our opinion matters more than others. The irony is that in many situations attaching 'star status' to a fund manager in itself is wholly inappropriate. Many of the biggest names shun the public spotlight and in some cases prove to be introverted personalities. This phenomenon is also strangely British and I don't pickup quite the same misplaced nepotism among European, US and Asian peers.

Whilst there is frankly no replacement for time in the field when it comes to assessing fund managers, yet I cannot call any a friend and only a few 'acquaintance'. That does not trouble me nor should it. They are my suppliers; they supply my investors with returns from their funds. I assess their ability to keep doing exactly that with reasonable risk and consistency. Conversely, marketing and media build an empathy and familiarity between the manager and the investor on the street, which is completely synthetic, contrived and disingenuous.

Reputations are mostly built on track records; the all-elusive alpha. Many among us follow fund managers not on the premise of what they have done recently but our bias towards what they did 10 years ago, how well a fund meeting went or the perceived charisma of the manager. Funds grow then attempt to manage the excess inflows. The greatest act of cynicism I have witnessed is the marketed 'soft closure' to new business, as a profession we do ourselves no favours by being seen to hurtle yet more assets at a closing door. It is perhaps the greatest marketing ploy drummed up by fund houses in recent years and fund buyers only seem to question capacity once having placed their ticket. If this appears to you to be herding mentality then I would say there is evidence to support that hunch. The FCA issued in April 2013 one of its occasional paper series ('Applying behavioural economics') on cognitive biases, and also concluded that fund investors tend to place too much bias on (a) over-extrapolation of past performance and (b) likability 'choosing a fund manager simply because we like the cut of one's jib'.

> *Wikipedia states that the cut of one's jib refers to: 'From maritime traditions, alluding to the identification of far-off ships by the shape of their*

*sails, as in the Naval Chronicles (1805) 'From the cut of her sails an enemy.' Used idiomatically of a person from early 19th century, attested 1824, possibly influenced by similarity of triangular jib sails to a person's nose.'*

Performance Half-lives. The last few years have reminded me of the start of the millennium; not in the sense of market returns, you understand (perhaps 2015 will prove more akin to 2007), but in terms of the number of fund manager moves. I recall the high number of fund managers suddenly wanting to pursue theology and worthwhile vocations. Before 2.0 there was the Aberdeen fragmentation following the split-caps debacle, the Invesco takeover of Perpetual, the end of Edinburgh Fund Managers, the birth of New Star and so on. Then I was a fresh-faced fund analyst in awe of the star managers of the day, in-taking manager moves on a new website called citywire.co.uk like it was Red Bull (first created in 1987). Like then as now, fund manager moves occur for a number of reasons but mostly from merger and acquisition, restructures, competition, retirements, promotions and individual values (the 'I suddenly want to focus on alpha from a Cayman domicile' symptom). It is fueled by ambition and wage inflation in the asset management industry; itself natural, cyclical and healthy. The rub is that earned reputation encourages fund manager moves and the more often a fund manager moves then the less reliable the extrapolation of their track record becomes. Past performance has half-lives; its value deteriorates the more times a fund manager moves or the environment around him changes.

Once a decade, a year comes along where fund manager moves appear to spike. These moves are often catalysed by a big event: in 2002 it was the dot-com blow-up; post 2013 it seems to be the two-pronged onslaught on fund fees coming from the Retail Distribution Review and broader move to passive investing. The underlying theme is a breakdown of trust between fund manager and investor and like any good spy film there are plenty of villains to choose from. Euro regulation of remuneration suddenly had an unwanted consequence of wage wars and creative equity packages. One move led to another, and then another in one large domino rally of well-cut suits and black polished brogues.

Neil Woodford (Invesco>Woodford/Oakley): The biggest fund manager move for a decade; we have seen much said and written about Woodford but I prefer to look beyond the man to the team left behind, which has good strength in depth in the likes of Mark Barnett. Whether Barnett can handle £30bn is not a question we seemed to ask Woodford when we as an industry channelled money into Invesco (perhaps itself a reason for Woodford's own decision to start again at Woodford). Rather than follow the herd into Woodford's new offerings; I want to work with Invesco to tackle some of the structural issues such as capacity, yield, unlisted positions and the near mirror that has existed between Income and High Income funds for some time.

Euan Munro (SLI>Aviva): Munro has created the most successful multi-asset business in UK history; his appointment to lead Aviva investors is justifiable reward. Frankly there have only been two choices with GARS, compete or jump on. Many have opted for the latter and it has quickly grown assets. Some who competed have been very successful in their own right; other less so. In terms of the man, Munro's legacy is assured but I am left in no doubts that the MAI team (under the helm of Guy Stern) had long since overtaken the individual and this applies similarly to the earlier defections of Batty, Jubb and Millar to Invesco.

Anthony Nutt (Jupiter>retirement): An equity income manager I had personally respected for many years for his considered almost bond-like (fixed income) approach; Nutt was already under pressure on performance including Sanlam's 'Black list' when he decided to retire and handover to Ben Whitmore. Ben Whitmore is definitely worth watching, his Graham & Dodd approach to value investing, eye for special situations in his two valuation screens and equity income experience going back to Schroder, promise a turnaround.

Richard Buxton (Schroder>OMAM): It is hard to say anything about Buxton not already stated. Here is 'key man risk' in its truest sense, by all accounts single-minded, idiosyncratic and decisive; it was the sequential departure of Errol Francis that destroyed any chance for continuity of the Buxton process. This actually sells Schroder's strength in depth far too short and overlooks underrated and talented managers like Sue Noffke. Schroder also has an ace card in the form of the Cazenove merger and the new managers that brings to Schroder investors like Julie Dean and Alex Breese; not to mention Phil Matthews poached from Jupiter (himself one of Ben Whitmore's alternates for his income fund had he stayed). Dominoes.

Epilogue: How effectively a fund performs derives from a number of factors and rarely just the individual: these factors are dynamic and the right balance feels like alchemy at times. As fund houses look to reduce their operating bases to meet new cost challenges head-on then I expect to see more careful fund manager eco-systems disrupted. In an age where we are increasingly sceptical of past performance then we need to look beyond the 'star' status of fund managers and become more questioning around 'key man risk'. Is a fund's success hinged on the 'key man' or is it the process, the team, the support systems? It's not Gorky Park! *#keymanmisnomer*

## CHAPTER 7 ▌ SUPER-TANKER FUNDS

*Liquidity Issues in Shallow Waters?*

Update: Roland Meerdter's Propinquity consultancy indicated that there were 634 'mega-funds' globally in Q2 2016. Those with $5bn under management or more. That's less than 1% of the fund universe controlling 45% of investor assets. About $10.2 trillion. We discussed in chapter 4 how regulation and industry forces were driving asset concentration at the group level, what about at the fund level? What are the consequences of BIG?

Rewind. On a return flight from Zurich to Heathrow, January 2014, I had an opportunity to reflect on an excellent conference at Davos. It wasn't only the mid-flight turbulence that had been a bit choppy. The mood during our Association of Professional Fund Investors (APFI) panel session was one of how to decipher the growing concentration of funds under management (FUM) in the fund industry and what that ultimately means for investor and fund selectors. In the UK we see ourselves as something of a big deal in European terms; the second largest mutual fund market. However, in global terms we are a very small pond indeed. The UK also has its strong proponents for buying British multinationals and thereby accessing the world. This is true but more consideration should be given to the liquidity of the issuing UK markets:

During the flight the BA breakfast was typically

continental. No beans, sloppy scrambled egg and that noble British tradition of chasing the mushroom here. No! Instead we were treated to the most continental of post credit crunch fusion food ■ the bacon croissant. A food item so lacking in single national identity that it can only truly call 'home' as 38,000 feet up in the air. I promptly rectified this by then having the traditional steamed egg, bacon, sausage, tomato and mushrooms on the subsequent connector from Heathrow back to Edinburgh. I chose to later skip lunch.

Today's globalisation is a strange dichotomy of the pursuit to make things simultaneously big and small ■ the macro and the nano. The funds-world originally aspired to be innovative and nimble but through five years of Darwinist investing today's most successful funds (commercially) have grown into the super-tankers of our time. The last 10 years has witnessed a series of severe liquidity crunches, which have discredited the long-held notion of market equilibrium and stable liquidity; coupled to a growing concentration of UK assets into a shrinking number of super-sized funds. The Alternative Investment Fund Manager Directive (AIFMD) and on-horizon UCITS regulation is forcing fund managers to reconsider the liquidity of their funds. This chapter examines the different strategies employed by oversized funds and how that has a bearing on their trading capacity and long-term viability. The chapter attempts to do this through making analogies between the growth in super-tanker displacement; draft, and hydrodynamic issues arising from large mass and low inertia, with the growth in fund sizes and resulting trading capacity and liquidity challenges incumbent.

Is Big Best? Today referring to funds in excess of £1bn funds as 'super' seems almost banal. Indeed the game has moved on as market capitalisation has grown multiple times since the dot-com crash. According to a PwC report, in 2012 the asset management industry is expected to break $100trn globally by 2020. In 2012 36.5% of assets were held by pension funds, sovereign wealth funds (SWFs), insurance companies and mass affluent or HNW clients. PwC believed this figure could rise a further 10%, representing a total of $130trn in global AUM. With that growth in capitalisation we have had to adjust to what 'big' means, now the biggest home-grown strategies like 'GARS' are north of £50bn (across various markets) and even equity income strategies like Woodford's peaked over £35bn before he announced he was launching his own firm Woodford Capital. As a fund market we have never really got used to super-sized funds yet in the last five years we have thrown our assets increasingly at a smaller number of funds.

Growing up in the 1970s, my dad was an engineering officer in the Merchant Navy and as such I was used to various anecdotes about his life at sea and what super-tanker leviathans were like to control. You see my dad worked on the very largest super-tankers of the day, known as 'Very' and 'Ultra Large Crude Carriers' (VLCCs and ULCCs). Indeed super-tankers have never been quite so large since. I was reminded of his stories when I started to first use the term 'super-tanker fund' to describe the rise of the many multi-billion funds (in excess of £5bn or even £10bn) that have become commonplace today. I'm not sure who first coined the term 'super-tanker fund'; it may have been me, but I don't recall anyone using it openly as I have done of late. The closest I came has been an old 1998 IPE article on Denmark building 'super-tanker' pension funds. Therefore in absence of specific objections then I will herewith drop my anchor and claim it.

Rewind a decade and any fund over £1bn was considered big news. Whilst at Franklin Templeton I tracked those among our funds, our '$1bn club', that were over that size. The reason I tracked these funds was for two reasons: (1) any signs of falling performance as the funds as has been subsequently captured by 'Active Share' studies by Patijisto and Cremmer (2009) and (2) for any rise in redemption risk based on the type and size of clients buying the fund. The bottom-line was evaluating how concentrated/diversified our offering was and therefore whether it was becoming more or less susceptible to flows into a smaller number of funds.

Turning my thoughts back to the size debate then specifically the growth in mega-sized funds has been heating up and rightly so. If we choose to liken funds to ships then the largest would most certainly resemble the largest super-tankers or crude carriers. If this analogy holds then the biggest risk for these funds is 'draft' and 'shallow water', let me explain. Draft is the naval term used for how deep a ship's hull sits in the water. When super-tankers are fully laden they sit very deep in the water indeed. Draft creates drag and this has a bearing on how ships handle in different depths of water. The study of which is called 'hydrodynamics' and super-tankers have long struggled with navigating 'shallow water', especially when carrying large loads of crude, gas and other commodities.

Hydrodynamics and Shallow Water ▪ liquidity as a function of price? Enthused by my analogous thinking I began to Google for relevant studies into super-tanker hydrodynamics. I found an old article called 'Ship Traffic Control: Controlling Ships in Heavy Traffic' in Mosaic January 1975. The article discussed the growing size of 'deep-draft' ships, or super-tankers to you and me, and the lack of understanding of how they handle, especially in shallow water and the rise in harbour collisions. The main problem is one of size and that super-tankers were built with cost rather than nimbleness in mind. The Mosaic article noted that super-tankers tended to 'yaw' rather than steer like conventional ships. Yaw is when the entire body of the ship moves sideways; often the rear adopting an attitude angle greater than the front of the ship as it is trying to turn. This is not an easy concept to fathom unless you see it first-hand. In investment terms the analogy is similarly challenging but it would be similar to, say, when a very large fund tries to dump a large amount of its assets into the market through program trades. As the fund exerts a large impact on the trading volume (and hence price) then the order book moves around the fund as much as the fund is able to get in and out of the market. Quite often there are insufficient participants to trade the other side of the book with the fund manager. The fund manager is then forced to trade out/in progressively and thus has to accept the shifting price (yaw) on day three in response to his trading on day one.

> *Super-tankers have no need to hurry, usually plowing along at 16 knots. This makes the trip from the Persian Gulf to Europe a month long, but keeps fuel costs down to about $150,000. Even at 16 knots, masters must peer far ahead for safe passage. If a super-tanker master orders "full astern!" from this speed for a "crash stop," as the rules of the sea dictate and admiralty courts demand, his ship will not stop dead in the water until it travels another three miles or more in some 20 more minutes. Moreover, because engine reversal destroys rudder effectiveness, the ship will usually slew, like a car skidding on ice, up to several thousand feet to one side or the other of its original, straight-line path. In turning, however, the yawed hull creates considerable additional drag, which slows the ship sharply. Such a turn requires more room for super-tankers than for conventional ships simply because they are so long.*

The Mosaic article also discussed the difficulties super-tankers have in shallower water especially and that many harbours in the 1970s could not accommodate these leviathans. The comparison to the size of some funds like M&G Optimal Income which controls nearly half of its tradable market is a stark one. The lure to compare the depth of liquidity and water is tempting. The effects of shallow water:

> *The fact is, however, that shallow water produces dramatic changes in hydrodynamic characteristics and ship handling. The effects are first noticeable at about three times ship draft (or 180 feet for a 60-foot-draft ship) and become pronounced at 1.4 times draft (about 85-foot depth). This makes even the English Channel shallow for some ships; 326,000-tonners avoid it, skirting the north of Scotland from the Persian Gulf to Rotterdam. And the million-ton tankers due on the oceans soon, with their 120-foot drafts, will render most continental shelves "shallow," often putting these ships in "shoal waters" while still hundreds of miles from land.*

> *The reason ship performance degrades in shallow water is the hydrodynamic interaction between seabed and hull. Masters and pilots notice two key effects: increase of directional stability and "squatting", riding substantially lower at the bow.*

This is where the Mosaic article really got interesting from a liquidity perspective. We see interesting phenomena such as banks reducing their proprietary trading to meet new regulation and capital controls. This suddenly removes some of the largest market makers in the space of five years since the crunch ended. Anecdotally this is beginning to cause liquidity tightening in various markets such as in bonds (according to fund managers) but the evidence isn't cohesive (yet) and regulators seem oblivious. I am now reading the Mosaic article intently; not because the issues were firmly concluded upon but rather that the timing of this article in the mid-1970s was asking the reader to reconsider what 'BIG' meant to the risks of navigation. For me this is preferable as I believe we are in a similar position with mutual funds today: when does navigating market liquidity become too onerous with growing capacity, when is big too big? The Mosaic article went onto discuss specific handling issues in shallow water:

> *At the conn, the sharp rise in directional stability shows itself in a turn, the turning circle may be as much as doubled. In part, this occurs because of the ship's "added mass," a fluid dynamics concept that refers to a part of the sea moving along with the ship. In effect, this gives the loaded ship greater inertia, resistance to changes in speed and course in shallow water than in deep.*

> *"Squat," like shallow water effects on steering, has been recognized for years but could almost be*

*ignored for smaller ships. However, with a 65-foot-draft super-tanker travelling in a 70-foot channel, it can be critical. The bow of a 900-foot-plus ship moving at 14 knots can be sucked down by as much as six feet at the bow, scrunching into the bottom. The degree of squat is related to the speed, so the solution is to slow down. However, as speed goes down, steering control, already more sluggish in the shallows, degrades further. The master or pilot must be prepared to make prudent compromises. Squat appears to be worse for full-form ships (typified by the boxy tankers) and is being studied.* ■

It is therefore logical that super-tanker funds can navigate larger; more liquid markets, more easily than smaller less liquid ones. This point has been drawn neatly into focus by the microcap unlisted positions in Woodford's super UK equity income funds, inherited by Mark Barnett in 2014. Directional 'Instability and Hysteresis' of big funds: the Mosaic article continued to discuss the handling difficulties that come from increasing the size in super-tankers.

■*However, because of its low resistance and great inertia, the super-tanker takes longer than other ships to respond to the helm. At service speed, the helmsman may set his rudder into a turn and wait patiently for up to a minute or two (and as the ship travels through its own long length) before the*

> *rudder forces build up sufficiently to overcome inertia to produce a significant change in compass heading. If engine speed changes are part of the manoeuvre, the wait may be even longer, some of the delay traceable to the time it takes propulsion equipment to respond.* ■

Here again we can make observations with some larger funds where the trading technology of the fund manager is comparatively slow to the volume of assets required to be traded. This can have a significant bearing on tactical asset allocation decisions. The Mosaic article discussed:

> ■*Many super-tankers have been found to have what naval architects term "directional instability," which means they tend to yaw without rudder changes. Some of this is good, in that it makes turning easier than for a ship with directional stability, which would tend to steam straight ahead. But instability also produces hysteresis, a lag in response to rudder reversals once the ship is into a turning manoeuvre, and a tendency to overshoot, or to turn more than the rudder setting would lead the helmsman to expect. The laws of physics also legislate why larger ships require longer to stop. Their masses (and, hence, their inertias) increase generally with the cube of length, but the resistance of the hull increases with only the square of length. 'In head-to-head passing, bow waves tend to turn the bows away*

*from one another. As the helmsman corrects, turning his bow toward the passing ship, and the two vessels' midpoints approach, pressure differentials tend to push them together, and he must turn away, taking care not to pivot his stern into the passing ship. Again, during this correction, opposite reaction will occur, tending to bring the sterns together, another quick spin of the rudder. Lastly (and weakest of all) as the stern waves react, they'll tend to push the sterns apart. One final correction.* ■

The analogy here is between super-sized funds (large inertia) and boutique funds (low inertia). By fact of owning so much of the market a super-tanker fund may become susceptible to unexpected 'beta' shocks as the trading volume around its positions becomes shallow and therefore even small volumes of trade can have a disproportionate impact on the price of its holdings. Imagine then when more than two super-tankers funds attempt to trade at the same time; and in the same direction, then the issue becomes quickly exacerbated. It has already been reported that super-sized High Frequency Trading (HFT) funds have helped to create 'flash crashes' when they have come into contact with one another. We recognise that order driven markets require plenty of both buyers and sellers; an imbalance of either will move the market up and down, to provide liquidity. This can happen rapidly and without warning and can become exacerbated if there is a sudden rush ('capital call') of redemptions. If the fund manager is unable to cover all redemptions out of his/her 'box' then the fund could struggle to find the necessary number of buyers at an optimum price. These issues will and do lay dormant for months or even years; so long as the market direction remains relatively straight-ahead. When markets become stressed and we see investor herding and asset rotations then these issues can suddenly emerge. As noted earlier large assets can provide economies of scale but can pose difficulties to navigate in difficult markets.

Super-tankers: The biggest? It is worth noting, at some point, my own personal bias towards super-tankers. Simply put I love big things: Redwood trees, blue whales, mastiff dogs, American cars, bomber planes and large ships. The world's largest super-tanker SeawiseGiant was built in 1979 by Sumitomo Heavy Industries, with a capacity of 564,763 DWT, more than 1500 feet long and a draft of over 80 feet. Draft is how deep the hull displaces water. This 'Giant' purportedly had a 339,500 sqft deck, and at her full load draft, could not navigate the English Channel. SeawiseGiant was renamed HappyGiant in 1989, JahreViking in 1991 and Knock Nevis in 2004 (as a moored storage tanker). In 2009 she was renamed Mont and sold for scrap. The sheer size of this ULCC is hard to visualise, longer than many of today's tallest skyscrapers. Yet ULCCs have never been quite as large since. As of 2011, the world's two largest working super-tankers are the TI class TI Europe and TI Oceania. Each has a capacity of over 441,500 DWT, over 1,200ft long, and a cargo capacity of 3,166,353 barrels.

Economics fuels size: Crudely put where shareholder returns are a function of earnings and operating profit for most fund houses today then if earnings falls in relation to assets then houses pursue scale, on a relatively fixed operating cost, to grow profits. A similar realisation was discovered by super-tanker builders over 35 years ago. The larger they are, the more efficient. In his book Supership, Noel Mostert pointed out that the 1967 cost for a round trip between Kuwait and Rotterdam through the Suez Canal on an 80,000-ton ship was $3.67 per ton of cargo. Then a super-tanker (say 250,000 tons) making the longer trip around the Cape of Good Hope reduced the per-ton cost to $2.40. As diesel prices rose then so too did the economies of scale for larger super-tankers as Mosaic wrote:

> *Ironically, the same reasons that make such ships economical to run are those that present manoeuvring difficulties and cloud their hydrodynamics. Despite their 1,000-foot-plus lengths and wide, blunt bows, they move through the water with great efficiency, with 80 percent of their bulk below the surface. Their drag, due to their length and relatively low speeds, is astonishingly small about 0.0005 of their weight. Comparable drag for other merchant ships ranges between 0.001 and 0.01 of their weights. (For railroad cars, it's 0.05; for a car, 0.07 to 0.1, depending on speed.) A super-tanker's drag*

> *resistance is so minimal, it has been noted, that if mobile on land, it would coast away on a grade too small to be perceptible. As a result, supertankers don't require much propulsive force. Most have very small engines for their size, because reducing the propulsion plant cuts the costs (about a fourth of ship cost is for propulsion machinery). Nearly all are single-screw and single-rudder ships. While adequate for normal cruising, they leave little or no margin for hard emergency manoeuvring. "Such an outlandish hull," Mostert says, "manoeuvred by one propeller and a single rudder, is, on the face of it, ludicrous."*

The interesting news was that for the first time the largest mutual fund in the world was passive (State Street's SPDR S&P 500 TR ETF) having overtaken then Bill Gross's mammoth Pimco Total Return Institutional Fund. This point is further hammered home by the dominant presence of Vanguard in the top ten, the US' largest fund manager. What jumps out, is that Sovereign Wealth Funds (SWFs) dwarf all but the very large mutual funds and ETFs. In the UK then certainly SLI's GARS and Multi-Asset Investment ('MAI') strategy stands out, no doubt helped by the rapidly expanding distribution in the US that is now overtaking domestic demand for the fund. Even Woodford's strategy, the largest UK equity fund strategy, would have been easily top 50 prior to his decision to resign but still some 20 times smaller than the Norwegian ULCC. Below I discuss some of the funds that I feel should be of interest to you in this debate.

Fidelity Magellan: The original super-fund; launched in 1960s Magellan's history is both long and chequered. The fund is currently only $17bn in size and invested predominantly in global equities. Once run by 'star manager' Peter Lynch until 1990 this was the first mutual fund to pass $50bn in FUM but has been in gradual demise for a number of years. Few UK investors will be aware of Magellan but most fund selectors do following the 1995 report by Professor Robert Bruner at the Darden School of University of Virginia. Jeff Feingold took over the helm, the fund continues to target the Russell 1000 Growth (like the Contrafund). Having trailed the benchmark for a prolonged period; the fund is showing signs that its recent nimbleness has started to payback stalwart investors.

Fidelity Contrafund: Fidelity's flagship was launched in 1967, weighing in at $75bn tonnes. William Danoff's fund is a global growth equity fund with a very heavy US bias; (around 80-90%) investing in some of the best known large cap names like Google, Berkshire Hathaway, Apple, Wells Fargo and Amazon. The fund's ten-year track record is up its Russell 1000 Growth benchmark but has underperformed over the last five years, thanks primarily to lagging in 2009.

M&G Optimal Income: Fixed income funds are generally able to handle large capacity due to the structure of the bond market itself. Whether this fully holds true for strategic bond funds; which invest more tactically between different bond sectors, is debatable. Other strategic bond managers have recently noted how Richard Woolnough's fund commands almost half of some of the sectors it invests in and accounts for 40% of the IMA Strategic Bond sector. His multi-million salary has been oft reported and questions the very efficacy of the AMC model. Back in 2012 and Woolnough reported that the rapidly growing size of the funds had made it more difficult to implement his investment views, but he had 'coped' with inflows. The tightening liquidity of the UK corporate bond market has been reported for well over a decade; a by-product of limited supply combined with over-investing by institutional investors. The fund has doubled in almost in the space of a year and the danger is that the fund lacks sufficient peers to be able to trade in and out of the market effectively. No surprise then that there was talk of 'soft closures' in 2012, which was badly handled by M&G in my opinion and only further accelerated inflows. Money Marketing ran a story (Concerns Grow on £11.2bn M&G Strat Bond Fund's 'Unhealthy' Dominance') on 4 February 2013 where FE Analytics indicated that over £3.7bn flowed into the M&G Optimal Income fund over the course of 2012 or 71.9% of the net flows into the Strategic Bond sector. Investment Week then ran an article on 6 February discussing the liquidity fears arising from 'big gorilla' trades and the unwillingness of some managers like James Foster (Artemis) to trade alongside larger funds like Woolnough's. In that same article Phil Milburn (Kames) noted that M&G could sell bonds to the Prudential if required as a result of outflows. I am left less convinced.

Pimco Total Return: Once over $200bn and the biggest mutual fund in the world, ex-Bill Gross' fund dwarves Woolnough's and commands huge swathes of the US bond market. Bond funds tend to hold far more issues that equity funds which is beneficial to running lots of money. Secondly bond funds tend to be run to a maturity profile which again is conducive to good liquidity management. Phil Milburn, co-manager of the £690m Kames Strategic Bond fund, came out in Investment Week in 2014 and noted that (then Gross) the fund owned a huge amount of the US index-linked market, which Milburn proposes was one the reasons why that market was weak the previous May; i.e. prompted by a sell-off by Gross. The counter-argument is that the fund is so dominant that it can effectively control the fund at will. However, I see huge redemption risk ahead for this fund, which saw outflows of more than $20bn in 2014 and significantly more after Gross' departure to rival Janus.

M&G Recovery: Tom Dobell's fund was renowned for being an active strategy, investing in recovering UK stocks and a fund I had invested in for many years... many years ago. Subsequently the Prudential merged a number of mandates and left the fund as a £7bn pseudo-tracker that scant resembled the original fund. As a pseudo-tracker the fund could be said to have sufficient trading capacity; as once a UK multi-cap fund investing in recovering stocks then the picture looks far less promising. This has seen the fund draw growing criticism, most recently from BestInvest's Spot the Dog survey where they labelled it as M&G's 'biggest mutt'. Although I am less than keen on BestInvest's far-from-high-brow analysis, I am also left in doubt over the structural integrity of the fund. From shore the fund appears to have found itself in unfamiliar waters with a leaking hull.

Carmignac Patrimone: The famous French based global multi-asset fund run by the 66-year-old Edouard Carmignac since 1989 has been one of the most successful funds in the cross-border space. The fund has traditionally benefited from gains made in emerging markets and it is here where the capital and fund flows have been reversed; reducing the liquidity in those markets substantially. As such this leaves the fund still able to trade in more liquid US and European markets but this in itself reduces the fund's opportunity set and ability to repeat past successes. The fund is currently allocated around 42% in equities, 51% in bonds and the remainder in cash-type assets. The fund's current GEM allocation is certainly less than in the past with around 12% in GEM equities and 16% in EMD. Performance-wise the fund has had a difficult couple of years and Carmignac Gestion has seen a number of manager changes at the start of 2014.

Aberdeen Asia Pacific and Emerging Markets mandates: Aberdeen has certainly felt the ill-effect in the slowdown from the commodity super-cycle and China. No doubt this has helped encourage a drive towards diversification through acquiring SWIP. At the time TrustNet reported that Devan Kaloo's emerging markets strategy was around £13bn. Analysts believed the SWIP acquisition would reduce the group's exposure to emerging markets and Asia Pacific from 40% down to about 24%, making Aberdeen Europe's largest asset manager, usurping Schroders. As it transpired, heavy outflows quickly scuppered such bragging rights. Capital outflows became the concern in Asia Pacific ex-Japan funds, Mondvisione.com reported in February 2014 that 'ETFs and ETPs in Asia Pacific ex-Japan saw net outflows of $1.3bn US dollars in February'. Meanwhile whenever founding father Mark Mobius ($13bn Templeton Asian Growth SICAV) gets on Bloomberg and talks about not buying into a GEM slide then I have reasons to be cautious. There is also a growing mood around the key man risk of patriarch Hugh Young; not helped by the poaching of the experienced Andrew Gillan, from his Singapore team, to Henderson and subsequent departures following the SWIP acquisition. Aberdeen continues to stress the team approach but most fund selectors still see Young as the firm's talisman. In 2015 Kaloo took over Young's role as head of equities. Talk of 'helicopter money' and the ups and downs in Japan ('Abenomics') may well encourage fund managers to rekindle a long-forgotten sector, Asia Pacific plus Japan!

Templeton Global Total Return: A fund I supported for many years whilst working at Franklin Ts (2003-2009) I have seen Michael Hasenstab's fund become one of the fastest growing fixed income funds in Europe, benefiting greatly with the strengthening sentiment towards emerging market debt. The fund can theoretically go anywhere but is hampered to the extent that Hasenstab tries to manage down his duration. The type and size of the markets are diverse, large and liquid albeit this fund is susceptible to tightening of liquidity in EM markets. Hasenstab (speaking to Investor's Business Daily in January 2014) said a big risk for investors 'was to do nothing' and urged against holding everything in cash. He has been fairly critical of the Fed, which is unsurprising for an EM-heavy manager. He is currently heavy in non-EU Europe and about a quarter of the fund in Asia with the remaining in non-US Americas, 16% in cash-type and only 75% in US debt. Hasenstab's previous active plays between USD and global currencies have slowed down with 60% of assets in 'hard' currency; the remaining spread evenly with a 20% short on the yen and 25% short on the euro. Hasenstab's fund has become something of a big super-tanker in the global bond space - it can and does invest mostly in deep water but some of its non-USD bets may be left in the shallows unexpectedly.

Standard Life Global Absolute Return Strategies: 'GARS' is probably the largest strategy in the UK today and has become globally significant. The total size of the strategy is oft debated and estimates range anywhere between £30bn to up to £70bn. The UK fund itself is over £20bn. The redemption profile of the fund benefits from the diversified investor base in the UK and overseas (John Hancock, CalPERS), strong internal proposition including

Insurance group and 'MyFolio' offerings. Liquidity, correlation and capacity are all actively managed and the fund has the benefit of investing in a broad, diverse and liquid opportunity set. The fund traditionally invested 70% into its internal long-only managers ('alpha buckets') but this has gradually reduced to about 60% allowing the multi-asset team to invest more in direct assets and derivatives. This is a very big ship indeed but one that can sail predominantly in deep waters.

Newton Real Return: In many ways the issues facing Iain's and Aron's Real Return are not dissimilar to Guy's 'GARS' but the Newton fund is much smaller and also less diversified, with a larger bias to global equities combined with a narrower application of other asset classes and derivatives. The Newton team seems adept in managing the volatility and liquidity of the strategy and gives me no cause for concern in terms of capacity at this stage.

Invesco High Income/Income: What is counter-intuitive and likely a function of growing size, has led in effect to the two flagship ex-Woodford funds being run as one strategy, with a very high overlap. Totalling over £35bn this strategy probably faces some of the largest liquidity questions today, from its small tail of micro-caps to large (≈10%) single positions in footsie names like GsK and AstraZeneca. Typical sizes of peer fund range from £1-3bn such has been the dominance of Henley's accumulation. The strategy is spread across the footsie and some of the FTSE 250. Nonetheless, the fund's large size and lack of nimbleness in finding yield has been called into question on numerous occasions. The departure of Woodford and succession by Mark Barnett was an opportunity to address the structural issues facing these funds. Woodford's departure has led to outflows and this may help ease some of the pressure going forward. Nonetheless this remains a super-tanker navigating in relatively undiversified shallow waters for its given draft. In 2014, Woodford departed Invesco to set up his own asset business. The move highlighted the fragility of star manager culture and super-tanker funds. The move leaves a legacy super-tanker at Invesco, now led by Mark Barnett, and Woodford's new clone fund, which is selling even faster than his first.

Fund draft and liquidity: how deep is the water? We could also examine the funds above by asset breakdown and then look at how much trading depth they enjoy. Let us crudely state this as the 'Depth Ratio', the sum of the draft (size of assets in each asset sector) divided by the total trading volume in each sector. The smaller the figure the more depth (on paper at least) the fund manager has to navigate his fund.

Draft in itself is an interesting nautical term; it's about the ship's displacement of the fund under the waterline. The larger the draft (for example when fully laden) the deeper the water it has to run in. The growing topic of liquidity risk has been brought rapidly into focus by the Alternative Investment Fund Manager Directive (AIFMD) which requires fund managers to manage the liquidity of the fund in context to the redemption profile of the fund's investors. This is a paradigm shift in fund management even if the industry hasn't fully recognised this.

Ask a risk manager how liquid his fund is and he'll say it can all (almost) be sold in a single day but at what price? In free economics then everything either has a price or it has no value. To have no value an asset cannot be reliably sold to a stranger. It is illiquid. Therefore liquidity is a function of price. Around this concept we have built a number of metrics to describe liquidity: resilience, depth, volume, spreads. The metrics are slightly different but they are interrelated. I will focus on 'depth' because it is the most nautical sounding and in many ways is the most useful because it accounts for the trading volumes and the effect on the price/spread. As a concept we can get our heads around the deeper the better. Therefore when need to have some understanding as to how liquid markets really are around the world.

Depending on which source you believe, the derivatives market in terms of trading volume and market volume is generally regarded the largest market in the world but its size is vigorously debated; the problem being the difficulty in sizing the many types of derivative market, covered, uncovered, contingent, OTC and so on. It could be as much as £500trn or even £1.2 quadrillion, which is more than 11 times the world's GDP. *Deeply liquid.*

The Foreign Exchange ('Forex') and related money

markets: Forex has traditionally been the largest cash market but has become increasingly driven by derivatives markets in recent years. According to the Bank for International Settlements, the preliminary global results from the 2013 Triennial Central Bank Survey of Foreign Exchange and OTC Derivatives Markets Activity show that trading in foreign exchange markets averaged $5.3trn per day in April 2013. This is up from $4.0trn in April 2010 and $3.3trn in April 2007. FX swaps were the most actively traded instruments in April 2013, at $2.2trn per day, followed by spot trading at $2.0trn. Core trading occurs inter-bank and between large investment banks and corporations, but we are also seeing a growth in small investor access and spread-betting through trading platforms like Prospreads, CMC, FX-Pro etc. Liquidity of courses does not necessarily translate to returns and the main purpose of these markets remains hedging and custody. *Deeply liquid.*

Equity markets: The total market capitalisation of all publicly traded companies in the world was $57.5trn in May 2008 before dropping to slightly above US$40trn in September 2008. Since then equity markets have easily surpassed their previous 2007 highs and generally considered to be the second most liquid market in normal conditions after derivatives. Therein the US equity market is the largest and most liquid, with the "Big Board" or New York Stock Exchange listing 2308 stocks and $16.613trn as of May 2013, with average daily trading volume of $169bn. NASDAQ with 2709 stocks albeit smaller by capitalisation (approx $4.5tn) remains far bigger in terms of daily trading volume ($982bn). *Variable depth.*

Compare this to the UK equity market. The London Stock Exchange has a market capitalisation of somewhere in the region of $3-4trn, making it the fourth-largest stock exchange in the world by this measurement and the largest in Europe. It lists around 2800 companies and trading volume anywhere between $1-2tn. Moreover depth varies by capitalisation and whether the mandate is constrained (e.g. yielding stocks). *Volatile depth.*

Bonds: Bond markets are even larger than equity markets but less liquid. Today the US is about 44% of the global bond market. As of 2009, the size of the worldwide bond market (total debt outstanding) was an estimated $82.2trn, of which the size of the outstanding US bond market debt was around $30-35tn according to the Bank for International Settlements (BIS) and the Securities Industry and Financial Markets Association (SIFMA). Nearly all of the $822bn average daily trading volume in the US bond market takes place between broker-dealers and large institutions in a decentralised, over-the-counter (OTC) market. A small number of bonds, primarily corporate, are listed on exchanges and this trend has been growing due to changes in regulation. Although weightings will change depending on Federal policy, it's not difficult to see from the table that the Treasury market is significantly larger than the asset-backed market. This has a bearing on liquidity all other things being equal. *Variable depth.*

Source: Wikipedia, as at 2011.

UK gilt market: According to the Debt Management Office (as at 06.02.14) there were about £1.4tn of gilts in issue, traded primarily by Gilt-Edged Market Makers (GEMMs) and a number of inter-dealer brokers. Through QE £373bn of gilts is actually held by the Bank of England; £370bn is held by pension schemes and insurance companies and a further £394bn of gilts is held by overseas investors such as SWFs. The remainder is spread across smaller holdings by financial institutions, corporations, local government, non-financial companies and households. The large holdings by the BoE, institutional and overseas investors and their often long-term investment horizon means that the liquidity in UK gilts can tighten rapidly. The DMO has been issuing a growing number of ultra-longs, which has helped the UK's debt position but may reduce short-medium term liquidity in the secondary market. That said, so far the DMO appears to have done a reasonable job in managing market liquidity but liquidity will remain sensitive to any slowdown in issuance and Quantitative Easing. *Moderate depth.*

UK corporate bond market: A number of studies on both sides of the Atlantic covered illiquidity in corporate bond markets as a result of the credit crunch. The lack of liquidity in the smaller UK corporate bond market has been often reported. The primary problem is one of institutional investors who buy up issues and hold them for long periods of time. A flat curve is allowing issuers to sell bonds at very low yields to maturity (sometimes below inflation) over extended time horizons. This reduces the roll-over and reduces short/medium-term liquidity in the market. Throw in a number of super-sized bonds funds and the trading volume plummets. Speaking in 2012 for an Incisive Media event, Kames Capital bond manager Stephen Snowden said liquidity in the investment grade corporate bond market had fallen 80% since 2007, which could create difficulties for managers trying to manoeuvre out of larger positions in this space. Liquidity issues can extend into high yield and index-linked. In 2012 the FSA sent a letter to corporate bond managers specifically quizzing them on their risk controls to manage low liquidity versus redemptions. *Shallow depth.*

Commercial property: As an asset class property is inherently illiquid but this can be mitigated through the long serviceable-life of properties, deriving rental income and managing the lease life and tenants. Property funds became very much the liquidity villains of the credit crises as they struggled to meet redemptions and imposed restrictions. Liquidity concerns in the commercial property market go back well before the credit crunch. Certainly not the first paper was Neil Crosby and Patrick McAllister of Reading University who published a paper a number of years ago, which captured the earlier work of many observers. Today I focus on the Jones LaSalles UK and European reports and compare this to the portfolios of direct property fund managers. The liquidity of REITs and real estate equity is then more complex but they share a common denominator. Through the crunch we saw REIT liquidity shrink rapidly and volatilities jumped significantly. It taught us that liquidity is dynamic to flow, volume, size of trade, price equilibrium of the order book and market makers. It taught us to not assume the old rules of liquidity apply all of the time. Remember that these are the sizes of the entire markets, which encompass millions of investors and broken down into ever smaller sub-sectors. It is in these sub-sectors where liquidity can become more dynamic and unpredictable and require your attention. Where trading volumes indicate shallow markets then low liquidity often equates to less resilience to market 'crunches'. Liquidity is no longer thought of as a constant and is something that requires active management and controls. The upshot is that large single asset class fund managers will face periods of liquidity tightening at some point in the cycle.

When do we know big is too big? This in itself is a difficult question and more easily established empirically than through modelling, given how dynamic modern fund markets are. That's the rub. A decade ago the adage about selecting fund size was simple - small equity funds good; big bond funds good and the opposite... bad. The rationale being that equities were and remain mostly secondary traded and so suit nimbleness; bond funds were mostly placed on the primary market and larger bond managers could control those placings and enjoy preferential yields. Now things are much more 'muddy' and the old rules are rarely mentioned and the era of the super-tanker fund is upon us; much like the 1970s and 1980s were the era of the super-tanker ship. The 1975 Mosaic article discussed how ship builders at that time did not have reliable data to know when increasing ship sizes were losing structural integrity, until it was too late.

> *The evolution of super-tankers, however, was originally an extension of the technology of their tinier forebears. As Mostert notes, in the '50's and '60's, they shot from 25,000 to 50,000 to 100,000 and 250,000 tons simply by strengthening and lengthening parts proportionately. Little engineering experimentation or design testing by models was undertaken. But then, others have noted, in the late '60's, the "rules," now in the form of computer programs for ship design, "began giving nonsensical results." There were reports of some of the newer super-tankers, then reaching 250,000 tons, cracking up and sinking, at least one directly after launching. Shipyards and ship buyers sent naval architects packing to their towing tanks, notably in Japan where the most intense super-tanker construction was taking place.*

In many ways today's super-tanker funds are built on yesterday's rules; they were never designed to be so large at outset but have since been adapted to handle high inflows and additional capacity. Some strategies appear to have been better designed than others and there are a variety of signs to indicate if the structural integrity of the fund has been compromised: slowing performance, rising volatility, capital loss, dilution adjustments, swing-pricing, long portfolio tails, increasing fund outflows, increased correlation to the benchmark and so on. Proponents of super-tanker funds will rightly note that investment banking tends to deal in even larger numbers and while agreeing this to be true the basis of investment banking is completely different to asset management and as such the liquidity challenges for investment banking are very different indeed. What is clear is that even our largest UK funds scantily measure as 'BIG' in global terms. Even funds like Standard Life's GARS and Woodford's funds are dwarfed by the largest passives from State Street, Vanguard and Pimco's Total Return fund. Put them next to the world's largest family office and sovereign wealth funds and they look very small indeed as the table above illustrates.

Does it matter how large a fund is? The answer is clearly yes because of liquidity risk. Liquidity management therefore has two aspects: the first is at the bow of the fund: how much funds flows are coming in and need to be allocated; the second is at the stern: how much funds flows are leaving the fund and require the fund manager to meet either with cash or by selling assets. The greater these flows become the more liquidity the manager needs from the market - thus where the fund invests is directly proportional to how much assets the fund has capacity for.

A fund can both diversify the liquidity through a range of markets (preferably low correlated) but also manage the liquidity as it deepens and shallows and correlations move towards and away from a delta of 1. This in many ways is not that different to nautical navigation where captains used sonar to monitor the depth of the seabed below them and changes in currents. It is not such a leap of faith to appreciate that large scale QE can quickly disrupt normal patterns and markets begin to take their eye off the readings. Ping... Ping... Therefore when considering the return prospects then consider first looking at the liquidity and depth of market beneath the fund to assess if the fund had adequate trading capacity.

*Fig. Fund Capacity relative to Trading Volume of Markets Invested: my hypothesis is that funds that are invested in markets with below £1tn trading volume will likely encounter capacity issues once they cross £10bn in size (if not before).*

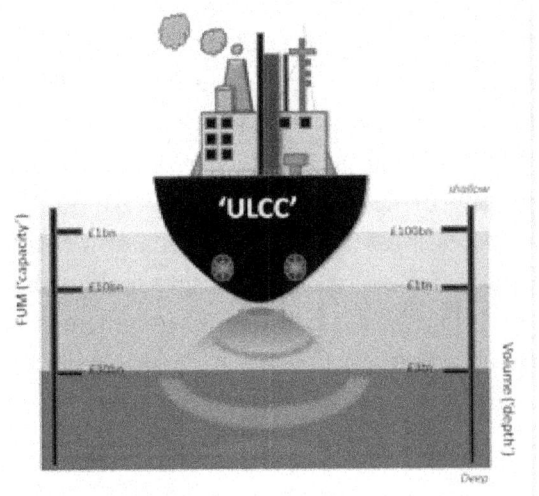

All Aboard? In many ways even our largest UK funds are not 'super-tankers' in comparison to the largest in the world. The problem instead is our fixation with domestic assets and the lack of relative liquidity (globally speaking) to support large fund sizes. Concentration of assets in a shrinking number of super-sized funds is bad both for healthy trading conditions and long-term competition. This is especially so when we fully understand just how shallow our markets are at home. Liquidity management has a number of interesting features; there is of course a time horizon consideration. Longer maturity assets require less short-term liquidity by function and this is why we quiz fund managers to provide increasingly detailed 'liquidity ladders'. There is also a more complex element interaction and interconnectedness. Events in one market may impact another on the other side of the world via capital and fund flows. The current capital outflows from emerging markets is a good example. Liquidity can be abundant one moment; with deep trading volumes, and suddenly gone the next and the fund is left floundering in the shallows. The issue is not the size of the fund but rather whether it is sailing too close to shallow waters. Since the credit crunch the UK fund market has lacked dynamism as the 10 largest fund houses appeared to exert gravity over the majority of net fund flows. What we did collectively was to increase assets into an 'uncertainty' theme, moving assets from single strategy funds into multi-asset, dynamic allocation funds. Let's call this for argument's sake 'DAA' (Delegated Asset Allocation). Auto-enrolment (or 'AE') is then set to inject anywhere up to another £100bn into the

UK fund industry and this is a genuine opportunity for fund selectors to start moving assets away from the super-tankers albeit insurance companies 'default funds' and NEST will likely stifle attempts to introduce competition. We are not seeing a lot of innovation in tandem with AE.

One possible reason for the slowdown in innovation is that fund houses will expect to get a brief RDR 'windfall' as adviser legacy begins to trail off on average of 0.3% p.a. Trail will completely unwind by April 16 under what are commonly known as the 'sunset rules' but many advisers have or will change their fee models sooner. Where the fund house no longer needs to pay retro to an adviser or platform then this gives houses a handy 300bps to (a) be competitive but (b) enjoy a boost in earnings in lieu of fee unbundling taking full effect. Fee compression is coming and what will shorten this boost is how quickly distributors can negotiate 'clean' share classes and the platform war already appears to be gathering steam. The other reason is that most fund houses have or are developing their own multi-asset offerings in readiness for AE.

The key question here is how effectively can a fund manager manage the capacity of this super-tanker fund? Confronted by increasing assets a fund manager can do five things: close the doors, hold more cash, launch a series of funds of the same strategy, increase the number of holdings or increase the size of individual holdings. The first two options are commercially unattractive; the third obfuscates capacity problems but does not address them;

the fourth tends to involve higher costs in terms of resources and processes and is utterly reliant on a finite number of new ideas. The last option therefore becomes unavoidable and it is here where the fund manager has to manage liquidity risk. The answer is a function of diversification (how many different waters the fund can sail in), market depth (how large and deep is the water the fund sails in) and processes (how large is the fund's rudder) to make nimble tactical allocation decisions. Firstly a strategy that can invest globally in large sectors can run in deeper water to one that only invests in say only UK equities or bonds. That should be obvious and perfectly logical. Secondly a multi-asset fund that can take both strategic diversified positions and make tactical rotations is more capable to manage changes in market depth than one that cannot. Lastly a strategy that is able to employ a number of long, short, paired trades and volatility trades has more ability to steer around rocks and shallow water.

Doing the due diligence: Using the AIFMD as a template we can start to ask specific due diligence questions to assess the liquidity risk of big funds such as:

- *Outline any illiquid, non-daily priced or low volume assets held and how you manage these positions (e.g. direct property, unlisted stocks).*
- *What is the maximum size (capacity) of your strategy?*
- *Have you stress-tested the current*

*portfolio, the liquidity profile of your investors or subjected the strategy to liquidity scenarios?*

- *What is the maximum percentage of the fund's assets held by a single client and the ratio of retail to institutional clients?*

- *What has been the largest weekly and monthly outflow from your fund and what percentage of the fund did this constitute?*

- *Indicate your current liquidity ladder at normal prevailing prices – how much of the fund you can liquidate in one day, two days, seven days, 30 days, 90 days.*

- *Are there any sub-sectors where you own more than 10% of that market? Also detail the smallest market and holding (market capitalisation) you are prepared to hold.*

- *What redemption policies (e.g. unit cancellation, equalisation, dilution levy, swing-pricing) can you currently employ?*

- *Provide details of the liquidity of your portfolio, including the type of cash instruments held, trading liquidity of other assets and how quickly 75% of the portfolio can be traded out.*

- *Highlight and describe any holdings held currently (or previously) in the following: Gold bullion, Commodities, Exchange traded commodities, Traded endowment plans, Milk quotas, Contracts for differences, Direct property, Infrastructure, Cash held for margin requirements, Complex derivatives (e.g. OTC, non-vanilla*

*Swaps, Swaptions), Unlisted securities (including private equity, private loans).*

When fund managers face increasing inflows they often increase the size of individual holdings. This presents a challenge for the fund selector who must work with the fund manager to understand the liquidity profile of the fund and the redemption profile of the client base. One must match the other and this has to be discovered during the due diligence process. As fund sizes and regulation grow then we should take liquidity management and capacity much more seriously before investing in super-tanker funds and ask the simple questions: how diversified is the fund by geography of issue and asset class invested, how liquid are those positions, what is the maturity profile of those assets and what does the fund's liquidity management look like? Seeking out small boutique funds is a worthwhile and as yet often overlooked approach to liquidity and capacity management. If you are unable to be fully comfortable with these questions or resulting answers then pause before weighing anchor. Full Stop.

*#supertankerfunds*

*Fig. Knock Nevis vs skyscrapers. Source WikiCommons*

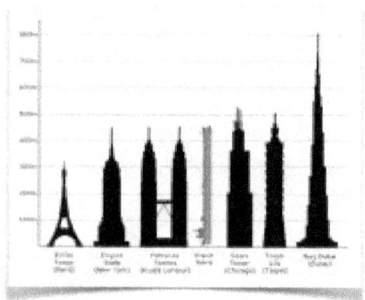

## CHAPTER 8 ▪ CORE-SATELLITE CONUNDRUM?

*Is 101 Asset Allocation Unwittingly Causing Asset Concentrations?*

Lift-off: Staying over in Westminster this week. Toolkit in tow I walk past the clock tower, Churchill memorial and the news crew (who camp almost permanently outside on the prospect of the latest political pantomime). I nod calmly and briefly to the policeman outside of the Parliament gates. I choose to ignore the young chaps who decided to incongruously sit in the middle of the junction to smoke their huqqah (hubble bubble) and dodge the mixture of tourists whom invariably stop abruptly to look up when Big Ben chimes. I prefer the slightly longer walk to/from Westminster station than Pimlico. During my latest tour of duty, I had been reading a lot about crowd thinking, crowd working, crowd funding, crowd shaping and crowd investing ... It is the new buzz narrative for how people may interact in a digital world and the prize of those who covet BIG DATA. In many ways fund selectors, unknowingly, have been acting as a 'crowd' for some time but not always in a beneficial way. Meanwhile a large ongoing debate is the survival of boutique asset firms versus the super-sized asset managers and is directly related to the way fund selectors allocate assets. This is something I see first-hand in my own work both as a gatekeeper, for a super-sized life and pension platform, and as a consulting CIO for a small boutique platform. Understanding why the big continue to get bigger; in the face of surveys that indicate contrary buying behaviour, is a key issue for our industry. I believe the answer lies in the traditional core-satellite portfolio model.

Core-satellite investing: Investopedia describes the approach as 'a method of portfolio construction designed to minimise costs, tax liability and volatility while providing an opportunity to out-perform the broad stock market as a whole. The core of the portfolio consists of passive investments that track major market indices. Additional positions, known as satellites, are added to the portfolio in the form of actively managed investments.' These days the core tends to be invested into a multi-asset fund or basket of passives. The wealth manager then invests the satellite allocation across a number of active managers to generate 'alpha'. The weightings between the two will vary from adviser to adviser. The key takeaway here is that the core allocation is more likely to be reused more often, again and again, and appear more frequently between advisers and wealth managers. Partly the reason is the delegation of advocacy among fund selectors, relying on the research of trusted parties to identify best fund choices to suit those core needs. To those familiar with game theory then in this instance there is a sense of advisers 'playing it safe' with the core allocation; seeking only 'alpha' through boutique specialists or higher beta ETFs. This is being amplified by the rise in popularity of benchmark-opaque absolute return, DGF, equity income and strategic bond funds. Passive assets have also been rising, supported by an array of active share and negative active fund research.

Unfortunately because of the 80:20 division of assets, fund selectors are unwittingly concentrating assets into cores while dispersing relatively little assets across the many. Here there is a mismatch between intention and outcome. Asset concentration is also being fortified by changes in legislation such as RDR, Auto-Enrolment and the de-annuitisation of the pensions market in 2015.

Group think: Despite a contraction in recent years the fund universe is still a big place offering investors huge choice and opportunity for innovation. Investing via a core satellite approach has been a mainstay of fund selection and multi-manager investment for well over a decade. Fund selectors often use such an approach to blend well-established funds with newer innovative boutique offerings. However, this approach has exacerbated the concentration of assets among funds and houses. There has been a growing commonality in the asset allocation to core funds. We have seen high mimicry among fund selectors and rating agencies. There is a high migration of staff among the ratings agencies and a large portion of the pension and financial advice segments rely on these agencies, while the buy lists of these agencies appear to have shrunk. The UK market has also become much more narrowly focused in contrast to cross-border funds since the demise of the offshore bond market. Generally UK fund selectors are buying more onshore funds than before and forsaking offshore options. A resurgence in investment trusts does little to offset the wider trend since ITCs are largely capital constrained vehicles serving the few rather than the many.

Thankfully changing adviser thinking shouldn't be as tough as Galileo or Copernicus convincing peers that the Earth did not sit in the centre of the solar system. Whilst attending an Investment Week 'Funds to Watch' fund selector event, I watched a boutique provider (Harrington Cooper) discuss how the results of their survey showed that wealth managers were buying boutiques over established players. The focus of the event was to highlight small satellite funds below £200m or so in size (surprisingly a few large firms (like M&G) lurked among the boutiques at the event). The results of the Harrington Cooper survey has certainly flown in the face of aggregated IMA data in recent years.

> *News release, 17 November 2014: 'Wealth managers to increase allocation in boutiques in search of more active approach'. Harrington Cooper.*
> *"41% of wealth managers and multi managers expect to increase their asset allocation to boutiques over the next 12 to 18 months. Only 23% expect to increase the percentage of their assets in passive funds. 95% of wealth managers and multi managers in the UK were attracted to boutique investing as they believed that smaller funds are much more nimble and able to adapt quickly to changes in the market."*

Other key outcomes drawn out by the survey included:

- *Interests of the investor and the fund manager are much more aligned within boutiques due to their small size (81% agree)*
- *Smaller funds are far better placed to deliver alpha (79% agree)*
- *Boutique funds offer a more active investment approach (74% agree)*
- *82% did not view brand recognition as an important factor when selecting*
- *Only 18% of those surveyed view a manager being star rated as important*
- *92% of wealth managers and multi managers look for funds with a high Active Share*
- *Passive funds were not as popular as boutiques among professional fund selectors with the majority (60%) only holding between 1-10% of their total assets in passive funds. Ninety-four percent invest up to half of their total fund assets in boutiques*

Harry Dickinson, managing partner at Harrington Cooper: "Fund managers are under increasing pressure to deliver value for their fees and people do not want to pay money to invest in closet-tracking behemoths."

The positive results of the Harrington Cooper study are a hoped signpost of changing sentiment, but is it enough? On the surface of this research the future appears bright for boutiques but the following factors may impede:

> *1. Large houses have broad offerings to capture shifting fashions and asset rotation*
> *2. Sample skew of the study, such as differences between multi-managers and advisers*
> *3. The persistency of star manager culture and brand advocacy*
> *4. Legacy fund compound asset growth outstrips new fund flow*
> *5. The rise of passive assets, which has been a disrupter for active houses*
> *6. The impact of RDR and Auto-Enrolment giving rise to 'default' funds*
> *7. False statements arising from negative biases embedded in the survey*
> *8. The influence of ratings agencies, consultants and gatekeepers, and*
> *9. Core-satellite bias, fund selectors leak assets into perceived 'safe' choices*

Eighty-Twenty rule: It would be nice to assume that buying patterns have fully shifted. It is more likely that a high correlation of fund buyer decisions are gravitating around 20% of funds with a much lower concentration across the remaining 80% of the fund universe. Like the formation of a natural satellite, gravity gathers seemingly independent assets together to concentrate into larger masses. Fund selectors are unwittingly concentrating assets into super-tanker funds and asset managers. Here is how:

> *Consider: Wealth Manager A who invests 20% of a portfolio into well-known Fund A, 20% into established equity income Fund B and spreads 60% across eight boutique managers. Wealth Manager B invests 10% in Fund B and 90% across a diverse range of nine different boutique managers. Wealth Manager C invests 50% into market leading multi-asset Fund C, 20% in passive Fund D and 30% across four different boutique managers. Wealth Manager D then invests 20% in Passive D, 20% in Fund A, 20% in Fund C and the remaining 40% in five boutique funds. This process continues, on and on, the individual allocations of the Wealth Managers appearing unique and diversified across 30 funds yet underpinning all of them is the investment, of the*

*majority of assets, into only four funds: A,B,C and D.*

Squaring the Circle: While these points may appear largely anecdotal; we can assess the growth of asset houses. If we look at the latest IMA rankings then we can see that the large houses are still getting larger and occupying similar market share to previous years. My 2013 paper 'Oligopoly Orchestration' indicated that on the previous trajectory the top ten IMA houses could occupy the entire IMA fund sector within three years. If wealth managers are now actively choosing new innovative boutiques, as the Harrington Cooper study would indicate, this trend may have slowed. One issue is that legacy ('sticky') fund assets are being compounded by continual regular premium flow and investment returns.

*Fig. An example core-satellite allocation: Source: 'Core-Satellite Portfolio Management' by J. Clay Singleton*

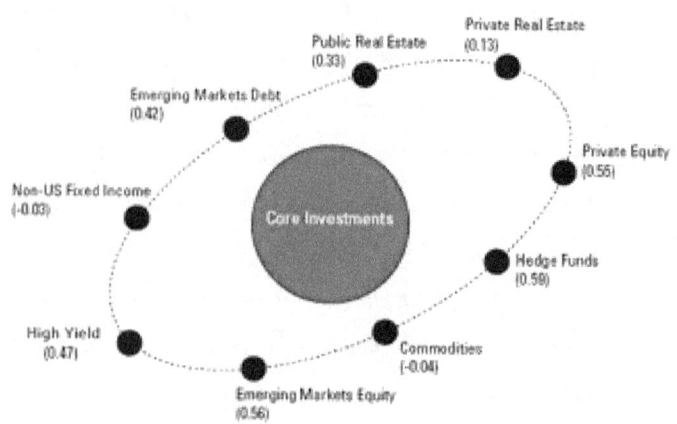

Compare IA figures from 2008 and 2013. Then the top ten largest firms controlled 53% of £660bn in September 2013 and 34% control of £500bn back in 2008. The trend growth in overall market share has thankfully slowed, albeit the figures were somewhat skewed by outflows from Invesco (following the Woodford defection). The fund universe has also expanded significantly since 2013, providing an opportunity for boutiques to reach critical mass, dependent on market capture from passive providers, merger and acquisition activity, market drawdowns or incoming global groups competing for the growing multi-asset sector.

Index insurgency? Belying the growing trend towards passives, there has been a group of Machiavellian businesses who largely stay out of the spotlight but now making supernormal profits. The index providers. Through global licensing the entire fund industry is now held to ransom to pay ever-exorbitant fees to these providers as a very quiet war ranges on between the likes of MSCI, FTSE and S&P. Giants like BlackRock flex their buying power as they did by famously moving from MSCI to FTSE. Most other fund managers are relatively powerless price-takers. There is clearly a mutual benefit between passive asset managers and index providers. The justification could be easily sold on transparency, the commonality of benchmark enabling easier comparison. Whilst that may resonate, from a customer perspective, it's not the driver here. In May 2015, the largest ETF index provider, MSCI reported that assets of ETFs linked to its indices grew more than 12% in the first quarter of 2015 to some $418bn. According to Investment Europe, around 56 products based on MSCI indices were launched in the period, which MSCI said was three times more than the next index provider. Where the innovation appears to be happening is in fundamental (factor) indices. MSCI reported 11 new factor index based ETFs launched in the period, attracting 31% of total asset flows to the category. AUM in ETFs based on MSCI Minimum Volatility indices hit $13bn. Assets in ETFs tracking the MSCI USA Quality index passed the $1bn mark. Meanwhile currency-hedged ETF assets attracted $28bn in new assets, half of the flows into MSCI Currency Hedged indices. MSCI said that there are 68 currency-hedged ETFs globally linked to its indices.

> *Following strong growth in the number of ETFs tracking our indexes in 2014, this year is off to a record-setting start. As the industry grows in size and complexity, we intend to maintain our position as the first choice of ETF providers who are looking for both leading-edge innovation and exceptional quality.* (Baer Pettit, managing director and global head of Products, MSCI)

Thinking back to that analogy of alignment I started with, we have to be mindful that consolidation and concentration is happening all along the value chain. Oligopolies already exist. It should be unsurprising (but suspicious) that among the largest producers of pro-ETF research are the index providers. Tracking the dynamics of the supply chain is as every bit as important as those parts, which are more visible to the end investor.

A universal problem? Not so long ago I was reminded by Shiv Taneja (then of Cerulli, then Strategic Insight etc) that the issue of fund market concentration is a global one. Back in the UK, the traditional core-satellite model (common in wealth management) likely compounds the issue of asset concentration despite the conscious efforts of wealth managers to allocate to boutiques. Asset expansion of the overall fund universe has slowed the market dominance of the ten largest groups but this does not necessarily equate to more market share for boutiques. This chapter does not deal directly with Active Share or the active-passive debate but does flag that passive assets are more concentrated (by firm) than in other fund sectors. The Harrington Cooper research gives cause for optimism but if we have already passed critical mass then simply changing new satellite decisions may prove insufficient. Instead fund selectors need to also seek new solutions to 'core' funds and address asset concentrations lying dormant in legacy portfolios. Moreover we have to stop thinking as a crowd and stop delegating away fund selection decisions to a small number of ratings agencies and gatekeepers. This requires better industry-wide adviser training and tools to select fund managers. On that basis, Houston, we have a problem.

*#coresatelliteconundrum*

# CHAPTER 9 ▪ ACTIVE v PASSIVE INVESTING

*QED: Are Fund Selectors Prisoners to Game Theory?*

I sit near St Paul's, in Paternoster Square, over a coffee. I sit in despite the bright sunshine outside, to save on UV cranium dome scorch syndrome. Outside is the usual bustle of sweaty brows, short skirts, Twitter frenzy and loud mobile phone calls. I have about 30 minutes before the next meeting. I am looking intently at the receipt I just received from the barista. £4.70 for a coffee! That leaves a whopping 30p for my lunch allowance, nice. I am well prepped for the next meeting, nothing too tricky today. With some spare time and a coffee comes an opportunity to think more about the active-passive debate.

Taking on the core-satellite question further, I examined the narrative around the active versus passive fund debate. Let us start with an obvious statement. If we all woke up tomorrow and the whole world had gone 'passive' then markets would essentially commoditise, as there would be an absence of price discovery. Price would be dictated to by the order book but free float indices would effectively lose their anchoring (devoid of any reliable valuation multiples). If you agree to some extent with that assertion the question turns to how do we fix active management? What research existed would be controlled either by the listed companies themselves or by the passive providers, which I suggest would be no good thing. I think we are all reasonably grown up and cynical of sell-side research to know that active managers play a vital role in sense-checking the bullshit that comes out of the Street. Contemporary conclusions by the Pensions Institute and the Local Government Pension Scheme had already cast a shadow over the use of active managers but does the issue lie with active management, sampling or cost? On empirical evidence alone, sales flows are telling us that the consensus already believes traditional alpha is a 'zero sum game' but also that SmartBETA and portable alpha (through absolute return funds) may have potential. The marketing machines of the asset managers are now focused on two sectors: index driven funds and multi-asset funds. However, are buyers choosing multi-asset for alpha generation or to delegate away asset allocation? Furthermore, what if we are looking at the active-passive choice all wrong, what if we are looking in the wrong places? The reality is that the risk of choosing active management invites the risk of choosing bad managers. Most funds are chosen by relatively inexperienced advisers; do more professional fund investors fare any better?

Prisoners to the tail? Why might buyers choose the wrong managers? Fund marketing creates perceptual context (or relative gaming) problems for selectors. Firstly it can skew perceived value for money if, say, a large group of sector funds are more collectively expensive that would otherwise be justifiable. Indeed we saw a degree of fees drifting up through the 2000s on a wave of star manager culture. Secondly boutique funds may simply be perceived less attractively compared to a well-known name and its accompanying marketing machine. A boutique then represents a risk (for the buyer) in context to a better known name. Fund buyers can be skittish beasts, they often need a lot of positive reinforcement in order to commit and hang onto laggards far longer than prudent. Both are at complete odds to alpha discovery. Ironic.Part of the problem is undoubtedly the past imbalances in marketing spend, broker commission and distribution reach of the largest houses versus boutiques. The other is that the narrative of 'success' has centred around chasing tail performance and related fund awards. The implication is that poor fund selection practices among advisers and flows to popular retail funds may have skewed the 'average' performance of active funds. In the previous chapter 'Core-Satellite Conundrum' I alluded that fund buyers may be falling for game theory by taking safe 'bets' into the same well-known funds. In other words fund buyers may be opting for 'safe' core options on an assumption of their inability to identify superior choices with certainty (see below). What economists call game theory; psychologists call the theory of social situations. Although game theory is relevant to games, such as poker, most research in game theory focuses on how groups of people interact. General equilibrium theory is the branch of game theory that deals with the economies of large markets between investors and manufacturers (in this sense of fund managers).

Keeping these concepts in mind for the fund market, fees

are now having a much greater impact on decision makers. Passive disrupters are setting ever lower fee scales, platforms continue to war on each other and large-scale fund players lower their charges in order to squeeze out smaller firms. When combined these behaviours have encouraged buyers towards low-cost and 'safe' existing names, over potentially superior new entrants, or in other words buyers have become prisoners to each other: better to be wrong together than wrong alone. We shouldn't also ignore that researching new managers is both timely and costly with little way of immediate incentive. One way for buyers to break out of these biases is to review core positions and invest into a broader range of active boutiques or innovative ETFs.

*Fig. Opting for the safe choice: are fund selectors falling unwittingly into a game of prisoners dilemma?*

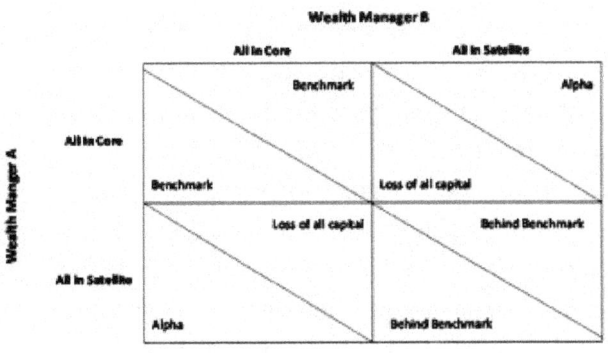

Can boutiques deliver better active returns than well-known super-tanker managers? The jury remains out. Day to day I observe that boutique managers more often operate like private equity managers: they buy companies not stocks; they finance businesses where they see growth; they have higher active share; they hold smaller capitalisation stocks; they hold for longer and they are less likely to buy the familiar stocks held by everyone else. Many boutique managers are self-invested and owners of their own businesses, which in turn builds alignment between investor and fund manager. Unfortunately few advisers and investors recognise the merits of such an approach, many prefer well-known managers and confuse unfamiliarity with risk and vice versa. To that end fund buyers have exhibited some game theory in their choices. On the other hand most fund buyers also know that a manager can perform best when given a small nimble portfolio with healthy cash flows to invest or a useful seed investment and the chance to soft launch the fund. Therefore new-start funds should be rightly approached with caution and size and pipeline factored into the fund due diligence. Perversely due to the growing asset concentration into super-tanker funds, many smaller funds remain small, at below £250m, and therefore present some useful longer term opportunities for the discerning fund buyer. Unsurprisingly the efficacy of active investing is dependent on approach and sector; there is no broad brush approach as many in the industry try to convince investors. Investors it seems cannot be trusted with nuances.

What about Factor Investing: SmartBETA or New Snake Oil? Factor investing certainly has many proponents like

Sharpe, Fama, French and my friend Dr Gabriel Burstein, but also its detractors, namely John Bogle of Vanguard and James Montier of GMO. There is a low-cost turf war between traditional index providers and factor index providers. The argument is whether the 'zero sum game' view for active management would also be true for SmartBETA over the long run. As one model out-performs; another will under-perform if we are to believe Sharpe. Advocates of SmartBETA insist factor investing is the best of both: avoiding the skews of the conventional market cap indices; with low turnover and costs. Ironically active managers also have the ability to change the tilts ('beta factors') in their portfolio to escape the same mean reversion, even if we are led to believe that few do so successfully. In game theory, SmartBETA may appear the attractive compromise to fund buyers wishing to beat the benchmark but unprepared to take a large bet against it. It may also just turn out to be the investment equivalent of the plea bargain, a compromised approach of return, risk and cost. Time will tell.

The ultimate expression of factor or rules-based investing are quantitative (or 'quant') funds. Think 'quant' and many in the industry may shudder, thinking back to black box strategies that contributed to the credit crisis in 2008 and 2009. The truth is that quant was never the problem; an over-reliance on numbers over logic most certainly was and so when selecting quant managers it is important to consider the manager as much as the model. Since the crisis and many successful quant funds have eschewed that moniker to focus on the qualitative aspects of the strategy, they down-play the quantitative component. Yet in a world of active share, smart beta and ambiguous style direction, pseudo-quantitative strategies are again finding favour, especially in the institutional space. The attraction is diversification and the promise of lower stable correlation and some downside protection from 'delta 1' events. Such claims rely on the robustness of each model, running multiple arrays of real-time scenarios and stress tests. The dubiety comes from a degree of scepticism that quant can deliver on such promises and indeed most fund literature now reads more modestly scribed than in the past.

The challenge for any quantitative manager is reacting to and timing market signals and what level of conviction should be applied. These are especially true in risk-on/risk-off ('ro-ro') markets. What may change going forward is that cross-sector volatility may begin to increase rapidly if there is a rate rise by central banks. This will test all quantitative models and I expect to see more discernible winners and losers over the next three to five years in much the same way as we did between 2004 and 2009. The important factor then is that these strategies tend to be atypical and difficult to compare yet many rely back on core models driven by external software suppliers such as Morningstar, MSCI Barra, Algorithmics, or APT. It is for this reason why the risk-adjusted profiles of these funds can gravitate to each other even at times the underlying holdings look quite different. In other words it is more difficult than you might expect to diversify away systematic (or factor) risk, especially during periods of market stress.

Surely US equity is the game in town? Contrary to expectation, active North America funds have continued to face difficultly in gathering inflows in the UK market, a stark contrast to (or perhaps because of) the rises in the US index, be that the S&P500, Dow Jones or Russell indices. One issue has been the highlighted under-performance of active managers, versus the S&P, coupled to the rise in benchmark products/ETFs. UK fund flows into US equity regional funds had remained subdued, since the dot-com crash, for over a decade. Interest, based on IMA figures, showed some pick-up in 2012 and 2013 but the vast majority of assets have been channelled into exchange traded funds like BlackRock (BGF/IShares), Vanguard and State Street SPDR funds (the SPDR S&P500 TR is the oldest listed ETF and famously overtook PIMCO Total Return to become the world's largest listed mutual fund). Between these three providers, and other passive providers, vast flows have been subsumed. This trend has moved across the Atlantic into the UK. At heady P/E levels, and sub-UK dividend yields, total return investors have remained cautious. Another major issue facing US equity funds, launching unhedged sterling share classes, is exposure to currency risk. Pre-Brexit, the long-run strength of the pound has long been a headwind for non-sterling assets. The UK and US economies are now disparate in terms of trade accounts: the US is close to being a net exporter, the UK firmly a net importer and this has a major bearing on monetary policy and approach to inflation controls. The unwanted consequence for the UK investor is that on a bid-bid basis the forex risk is passed on. At the time of writing, hedged share classes have become more popular and there is growing doubt over the validity of previous long-run currency studies (e.g. MSCI Barra's dollar-sterling study) against today's economic outlook. Interestingly UK investors have gradually migrated from UK to global funds; the question then is, what sort?

Global equity funds. 'Money is king' they say and the quantitative easing of Western economies and reversal of capital flows have dramatically changed the returns of global markets and global equity funds incumbent. At the time of writing it is too early to tell if Shinzo Abe hits the target with his third arrow or if Mario Draghi turns out to be super. Meanwhile the sector has witnessed a strong secular rotation in recent years: from an engine room powered by growing Global Emerging Markets (GEM) wealth; to one of capital outflows and Western retrenchment, recession, investment, recovery and return. This had led to a vast change in the competitive advantage between global equity funds. Whereas, until the credit crisis, the trend was one of increasing GEM exposure to capture 'geared' returns over developed indices; now GEM returns have trailed developed markets over the last five years. However, the macro drivers for GEM have not gone away; albeit slowed, and the previous 'de-coupling' thesis (otherwise referred to as South-South trade) is on hold rather than discredited outright. The challenge for the fund selector is whether to punish or to cut the fund manager some slack in the short term, while GEM markets recover, or tolerate allocation drift to defend performance. This also begs the question 'when is the right time to get back into GEM?' Having worked for a fund house utterly focused towards GEM equity, I have absolute sympathy for global equity managers who have stayed true to the long-term story. Unfortunately your average investor is somewhat less tolerant.

In terms of region specific funds, what does irk me is when a GEM, Japan or Asia Pacific manager says they are a stockpicker and yet spends half of a presentation covering macro 'tailwinds' or 20 year forward demographics. Fund managers can't have it both ways, either play the macro card or the company fundamental card and expect the fund buyer to have positioned accordingly. If macro is truly a component of the process, or to discern country differences intra-region, then fair enough but most often it's not the case. Advisers may lap up those sound bites; professional fund buyers need to assess what makes this particular fund manager different. It can all get a bit repetitive when you've seen 20 managers from the same sector. You list me in the first five slides.

Another point of investment debate is one of access ▪ how to profit from emerging markets while perhaps avoiding some of the pitfalls. This has emanated in two clear strategies: firstly direct allocation into GEM stocks and timing when to be in and out, and secondly, to invest indirectly through developed stocks and allow companies to decide the allocation of capital. Both approaches promise diversification, the first offers the less unadulterated returns but also volatility (price and currency) the second offers exposure but commingled with less currency effect and less scope for inefficiency in the market. Western stocks are monitored very closely and a manager runs the risk of not capitalising on the GEM story due to slowdowns elsewhere on the company balance sheet or 'crowding out' as investors quickly respond to reported results or new GEM-related deals.

What about Specialist funds? Sector specialist and thematic funds may capture factor risks unrepresented by traditional indices. Consider examples like energy funds, technology funds and frontier markets funds. Talk about energy funds and most fund selectors will still refer to them as being in the periphery. In many ways they are useful signposts for today's investor and potentially a useful diversifier for experienced buyers. What has lost favour is their attraction as dedicated investment themes. That may be missing a trick since energy fuels our modern economy and allows us to eat, move, work and interact in all facets of modern society. Consequently energy stocks will always display a number of market and geopolitical factors. From the slowdown of oil and gas, to the exploration of shale gas and the future of renewables. I don't currently invest in direct energy funds, it involves a call that is too macro for my liking. Superior management will invariably require the use of derivatives in order to hedge out some of the risks. Most funds will benchmark the same MSCI AW Global Energy index and this should be comparable (on paper at least). What makes the sector even more tricky to position is the complex competing supply chains between energy markets: oil, gas, shale, nuclear, renewables that are likely to exist for more than a generation. As such I am not sold on the diversification benefits, as correlations to other markets will likely prove transient. Given those market dynamics, if I did invest, then I would most certainly consider an active over a passive approach.

Then you have more esoteric sectors such as infrastructure, real estate, private equity funds. There is growing demand for investment to fill the shortfall in government and retail bank investment. The thesis for infrastructure is clear economically but unclear as an investment. This exposes the disparity between economic and investment cycles. Fewer and fewer investors are looking to cash match a long-term liability. If investors want to invest long-term then they want volatility to increase the risk premium. Esoteric sectors become increasingly attractive when the headline returns of liquid markets begins to run out of steam. Current core debt markets have horrendous expected returns. We saw similar phenomenon in 2005-2006 into REITs, collateralised debt with negative consequences. Floating rate and ABS funds are again popular and attractive for having lower duration to potential rate rises. Also, a secondary impact of duration is default and I think the indebtedness of the market is understated as is its resilience to rising interest rates. We may see a rapid growth in assets feeding into such funds through new European regulated European Long Term Investment Funds (ELTIFs). However, the premium from these sectors have to be approached with caution as liquidity can quickly change. My suspicion is that whilst appealing; they are simply unsuitable for retail investors from a liquidity perspective. They are best wrapped into institutional funds or closed-ended structures. The problem is one of leverage and investor redemption risk. For example where infrastructure leads to increased exposure to acquisition, development and construction loans then there is project, macro and refinance risk. For this reason there are quite onerous SEC Comptroller rules in the US, but the rules appear less explicit in Europe and the UK. This may lead to problems down the line. Similar caution has to be adopted around PFI-linked investment and renewables projects. For example infrastructure funding has yet to fully consider the impact of decarbonisation on the return of capital. That cost is set to rise. Meanwhile decarbonisation strategies are also attracting attention and may offer diversification benefits in a portfolio exposed to energy or infrastructure. There is also an inflation component that, frankly, the market hasn't figured out at the time of writing. Fund buyers need to decompose the potential premium for all of these strategies, over traditional assets, and assign a probability of risk to each then stress those through different scenarios. I expect serious liquidity issues will arise if ELTIFs or future UCITS rules allow increased retail investor exposure to esoteric, private assets.

Like many fund selectors, I am something of an ignoramus of sustainable investing funds but have a good friend and ex-colleague who is a lecturer in this field at Edinburgh University and I should be more interested. I recall at one event about 10 years ago that 150 leading fund selectors to zero voted against investing in Jupiter's then long-established ecology fund. Times are now changing because sustainability has entered through the side door of corporate governance (CESG). The dilemma ten years ago remains the same, either buy on prospect of better returns through Darwinism (better stocks evolve to new demands), diversification to lower correlated returns to broader markets or satisfy an environmental objective. The first two aims are natural to an investor, the latter is more reserved for what are called 'mixed motive' funds in the charity sector. It is possible to be green and still be healthily in the greenback? What is (slowly) changing my view are initiatives like the Portfolio Decarbonisation Coalition, a UN-backed, multi-stakeholder effort with an objective to lower carbon and greenhouse gas emissions across $100bn of institutional investment assets under management. Early adopters include the AP4 Swedish pension fund, non-profit organisation CDP, large asset firms like Amundi, Natixis and index provider MSCI. The guinea pig in this instance is the AP4 pension fund, which aims to lower the carbon emissions of its assets by 50-80% without impeding returns. The latter point is interesting to me. If the specially designed MSCI Global and European

Low Carbon indices are to be believed then being greener and matching the broad market is possible. The unseen but interesting sub-text for me then is what positive factor exposures enter your portfolio by seeking out stocks with lower carbon emissions: e.g. lower ENP exposure, currency, more efficient operating bases, or government incentives etc.

What about the next frontier? I am somewhat familiar with Frontier and MENA funds, having been involved in the launch of Mark Mobius' Frontier Markets SICAV fund. Originally the notion of MENA funds (like 'BRIC') was a convenient way to group a certain region of the world under a catchy macroeconomic theme, namely oil-induced revenue and wealth. Part of the allure was clearly a play by Western fund groups to appeal to Middle East customers, sovereign wealth funds and in turn sell back to the West as sentiment towards GEM spread into broader markets. In truth investment in the Middle East is nothing new; intensive since the 1970s, it is the vehicles of investment that have been changing and broadening. We see a variety of exposures among this peer group; a symptom of bouncing around inside the GEM super-sector, and some of these funds fly close to being country-specific funds. Country risk should definitely be on the table when discussing these funds. Emanating from the 1990s; MENA funds began to really spring up in the early to mid-2000s, the attraction was a diversification away from increasingly weighted traditional GEM allocations (the need to find new markets). Since the credit crunch, and in particular since the start of the China-plenum slowdown in 2011, we have seen a complete reversal in BRIC and GEM fortunes both in fund flows and performance. Given that most of GEM seems to carry varying degrees of correlation and reliance on the China story then it is understandable if investors may see MENA and Africa funds as an alternative play. My first niggling issue is cost, MENA funds are usually too expensive for the average investor, too firmly rooted in higher charges geared towards the Middle Eastern HNW buyer. Post-RDR and fee reform is absolutely critical if such funds ever hope to compete. Secondly, the Middle East cannot be considered a 'Frontier' market, not now, not then. That notion presents real problems for me and a trap for unwary fund selectors trying to draw comparisons with broader GEM funds. Perhaps 'fringe' rather than frontier would be a better description. Many MENA strategies are actually North Africa light, opting instead to take on exposure to Egypt and Jordan. The Arab Spring did much to unsettle investor confidence and this has generally driven MENA managers to concentrate towards OPEC countries. Is Middle East still an oil play? Clearly in beta terms the answer is yes. Many more industries have sprung up but the money trail (such as Financials) still leads back to the same origin. The geopolitical landscape of the Middle East is enduringly complex and there is a need to discern the level of geopolitical risk and global oil sensitivity a fund is carrying. Analysing correlation against just the fund's benchmark is not enough here. The last issue facing fund managers is the size of the investable universe; there is simply not enough quality prospective stocks to build core portfolios, as would be possible in Europe, Asia or the US. Lastly the USA's concerted move to immunise itself from OPEC oil, through shale gas, is a real head-wind if Europe follows suit. The Middle East, whilst wealthy, now faces the real challenge of slowing economic growth.

Africa remains the great misnomer, the misunderstood region, among fund investors. No longer termed the 'dark continent' in a post-PC world; it remains a blind spot for most western investors. Its potential is vast yet it is the most disparate continent on the planet: politically, culturally and demographically. To talk about an African strategy is akin to an Asia Pacific strategy but more disjointed between North, South, East and West and minus the strong inter-trade agreements that bind the ASEAN trading countries together with China. This has made it a challenge to all but a small few houses like JPM and Investec. Like Asia 30 years before, the long-term story for Africa is strong demographically; yet the timing of Africa's wealth explosion is neither agreed nor certain. A 20-30 year horizon may be too long for the average investor and there is no certainty as to what returns will be made in the interim preceding. One misnomer I see among Africa funds is a reoccurring play through South Africa, which (like Asia/Australia) I do not consider to be either an emerging or frontier market. That said, I can appreciate the returns on offer but best to check that you are not already taking that exposure elsewhere in your portfolio.

What of once-loved technology funds? They have been banished from mainstream investing since the dot-com crash and yet technology stocks are now among the world's leading blue chips, some of the largest capitalised companies and core holdings in a vast majority of portfolios. At an industry level it is ironic that technology funds have not shared in the turnaround more. Think 'technology' stocks these days and most will jump to name Google, Samsung, Apple or Amazon but the technology and broader TMT sector are much more diverse than that. Honestly, it is not a sector I have considered much in my day job, for nearly a decade. It is fair to say that most technology funds have had a tough run since the dot-com bubble burst over a decade ago. What rose out of the ashes was something of a new paradigm, an era of super-sized Web2.0 and next generation mobile device providers. No longer was the focus just Microsoft or difficult to value venture-capital Silicon Valley start-ups, and with that mainstreaming, technology funds were marginalised to the periphery. Many investors seem far happier to take a chunky exposure through all-sector funds or passives. That trend would seem to bear through in the numbers. The Investment Association has consistently reported flat to negative sales flows, reversing product development activity, fund closures and mergers. The IA onshore sector only lists seven funds according to Financial Express. I struggle to recall what the sector was at its height in 2000 but it was easily over 20 funds, perhaps even 40. We are thus not exactly spoiled for choice. Why then does it make sense to consider distinct technology funds again? Simply put, diversification. Super-sized tech stocks have all but lost their diversifying benefits by becoming large index weightings, the constant flow of liquidity drives increased sell-side research and that in turn starts to correlate large techs to the benchmark. It means a super-sized tech stock has little portfolio benefits over an auto like GM or retailer like Walmart. However, tech specialists will seek to capture emerging trends far earlier in the cycle and further down the cap spectrum. It is that discovery of innovation that can create positive surprises and lower correlation to the mainstream. Curiously the shrinking fund sector may actually allow tech funds to again find demand.

Alternatives ▪ Portable Alpha? Are then alternative strategies the answer for active management? If Long-only active is a 'zero sum game', what about long-short and portable alpha? Most studies are completed by academics, or consultancies, and rarely by on-the-ground fund investors. I know of at least one highly respected member of our industry looking into this very point and it remains one of the unexplained sectors within the narrative of the schools of Sharpe, Fama, French and contemporary luminaries. That said hedge funds have taken a battering both in lost AUM, poor performance, regulatory pressure around tax and poor transparency and widespread criticism over costs. What is certainly true is that the days of 'two and twenty' are well behind hedge funds (or soon will be). Most alternative UCITS ('Alt' UCITS') funds are managed very differently to offshore hedge funds but some still charge performance fees and annual fees in excess of 1%

are commonplace; my hope is that fee compression will improve outcomes for investors and provide an alternative to the mercy of index beta. Theoretically performance fees create alignment between fund manager and investor but the general mood is that they instead create excessive fees for the fund manager at the sake of the investor. The CASS paper on symmetrical performance fees is a radical proposal but one that captures the aforementioned mood. As stands, performance fees create a drag on a fund that might overshoot the target one year but then be down for the next two, and all the while could be trailing funds without performance fees. Recent scares of portfolio managers front-running in favour of books with performance fees only adds fuel to the fire. Where fees are addressed then the promise of capturing returns away from the market will likely hold appeal to buyers, especially where the cost of investment is deemed fair, proportionate and risk controlled.

Absolute and long-short equity funds tend to do best during periods of see-saw markets. Returns net of fees are therefore critical to long-short funds as there can be periods where markets are relatively benign as was the case through 2012-2014. When thinking about absolute return and long-short funds, firstly you have to suspend all conventional approaches to fund selection, chasing metrics like beta, alpha, tracking error and active share simply don't add up when working with funds that apply shorts, dynamically change style bias at will or capture stripped-out risk premia. As we mostly talk in absolute terms of performance; so must we in risk terms be that volatility, correlation, capture rates or drawdown behaviour. Some fund analysts still make this fundamental mistake. Instead, as a fund buyer you have to look through the portfolio, understand the strategies being taken, expected market direction, and economic exposures should all be anticipated through different market conditions. This may sound obvious but where the manager is shorting then understand what exactly is being shorted. Is it a clumsy hedge against a market proxy, a stock specific risk, stripping out stock specific risk from a market basket, a short against a factor risk like oil, inflation, volatility, duration, arbitrage or a valuation anomaly? Sometimes the answer is straightforward; sometimes not. The other consideration is the relative notional size of the short and long book and what that looks like in terms of overall net exposure. Lastly look at how the manager is achieving the 'short', be that physical short selling (non UCITS), covered futures, CFDs, swaps or options.

Whatever the approach, a key factor I look for in long-short equity (including 130/30 'xo/xo') funds is whether the manager is deriving positive 'carry' from the short book. Shorting has to be cost effective and the approach repeatable. If I cannot find that then I am more inclined to walk away. I have also observed that good long-short equity managers target their shorts at the stock level and make their long books and short books the output of one fundamental process. Others use shorting more technically, as a means to capture behavioural investing trends. Where

I see awkward examples is where managers try to hold long stocks and short indices, this invites basis risk and the result is you get more of a crude 'hedge' effect that actually capturing alpha. Consequently the most over-used but under-delivered term I hear these days from managers is 'asymmetry'. It is easy to confuse asymmetry with leverage. Derivatives tend to have a natural gearing effect due to the small nominal cost of the contract compared to its economic notional exposure. Delivering simply from leverage is fine but is not delivering asymmetry. Such funds often blow out during a 'delta 1' event and often far less diversified than the fund appears in normal conditions. Many funds deliver symmetrical returns to risk, which often becomes a 'zero sum game' in the long run after fees. Where managers are exploring price arbitrage then there needs to be evidence that the manager is able to sufficiently capture and close-out before the arbitrage 'channel' narrows and wipes out any gains. Many others take directionality even when they say they don't and so you have to understand the nature of the fund, especially if ever hoping to match to a client's risk profile or blend more than one together. This is a very different approach to traditional diversification. Asymmetry is often captured by a manager not deciding to short as much as when shorting. It is all about the fund's up and down market profile.

Uncertainty is the core utility behind absolute return funds. It is easier to understand its importance if you treat it as a theme, like ageing population or growing emerging market middle classes. Removing or controlling uncertainty carries a valuable premium to the investor. To this end, absolute return funds compete indirectly with structured products. Both are designed to deal with uncertainty, one implicitly, the other tacitly. Structured products have remained in the background of wealth management for many years, arranged as direct investment products for a range of investor types but rarely held within a collective. Indeed, permissible investment rules often curtail the holding of structured notes and products. The advent of structured product funds heralds the start of a new sub-sector of funds that ostensibly invest into indirect investments with structured payout profiles. Consider pertinent due diligence questions when using structured products. The nature of protection (be that a hard or soft floor), the trade-off between having protection and opportunity cost of lost market gains, whether to buy over-the-counter (OTC) or on-exchange, return expectations of the reference index, use of digitals (two or more indices), types of barriers used, whether the rate of upside or downside is leveraged, how often the product resets, the maturity of the product, whether the floor is ratcheted up, the prevailing market levels, counter-party risk, liquidity risk, market volatility, cost of derivatives, the underlying asset invested by the counter-party, the strike price and the cost. What can impact that cost is prevailing cross-sector volatility, which can rise on geopolitical turmoil in Ukraine, Middle East, QE tapering as well or changes in the cost of carry such as base bank rate rises. Unsurprisingly, the focus on the risk of index-based products has made products with built-in protection more attractive. Admittedly I have overlooked fixed income for now, the arguments at time of writing were far more structural and endemic than about fund selection.

If you pickup that none of the above appears straightforward then you would be right. The point I am trying to make here (in a rather long-winded way) is that many fund pickers are ill-equipped to choose the right managers and likely looking for alpha in the wrong places. This has been highlighted by Diane Del Guercio and Jonathan Reuter in their paper 'Mutual Fund Performance and the Incentive to Generate Alpha' http://onlinelibrary.wiley.com/doi/10.1111/jofi.12048/abstract. The study, published in the Journal of Finance, indicates commission-driven brokers may have been complicit in the poor 'average' performance of active funds.

> *'we show that actively managed funds sold through brokers face a weaker incentive to generate alpha, and significantly underperform index funds.'*

Where then does the professional fund selector add value? That's debatable. Fund analysis, for me, is far more about understanding people and processes than measuring performance or studying lagged data in Bloomberg all day long. If a fund selector cannot interrogate a fund manager face to face then they are in the wrong job, pure and simple. The old adage of 'never judge a book by its cover' is never truer than for fund selection. Marketing literature is largely the product of regulation and distribution. It is therefore an awkward combination of mandated content and that designed to sell the fund. Neither type is of much use to the professional fund buyer, who is always trying to discern between manager A and manager B. Risk warnings, yada yada macro slides, simplistic process flow diagrams are ostensibly decorations. Instead the fund selector adds value by gaining better access to fund managers, asking the tough questions, discussing trades line by line, understand the motivations, lobbying fund managers on behalf of investors, putting pressure on fees, engaging corporate actions and taking a clear view. In younger analysts I look for a healthy dose of cynical curiosity but rarely find it. Suffering splinters by sitting on the fence helps neither fund manager or the investor. Managing one's own biases is a constant challenge. That includes meeting head-on both active and passive funds.

So where does this leave us? The active-passive debate has cut the fund selector community right down the middle, with polarised sides and the majority of selectors now buying both to a greater or lesser extent. The biggest issue is that many studies simply do not take into account active fund selection, variability of time horizons, alternative strategies or portfolio diversification. Related issues include level of fund fees, performance fees, regulatory changes, contraction of the fund universe, asset management earnings, growth in size of portfolio teams, asset management and wealth M&A, asset concentrations, rise of super-tanker funds, role of boutique managers, core-satellite investing, performance persistency, performance presentation and active share lore. In 2015 I created a questionnaire, ten questions to around 100 fund selectors for their views on active funds, passive funds, fees and related topics. Some of the key outcomes of the survey included:

> *1. 73% of respondents felt passive funds delivered better than active funds, most or some of the time*
>
> *2. 89% of respondents felt high fees prevented active funds from beating passive funds, again most or some of the time*
>
> *3. 60% of respondents felt boutiques deliver better than super-tanker funds*
>
> *4. 85% of respondents felt an AMC of 0.5-1% was reasonable for active funds*
>
> *5. 58% of respondents employed some form of core-satellite allocation*
>
> *6. 63% of respondents felt star manager culture perpetuated active funds*
>
> *7. 52% of respondents felt SmartBETA (fundamental) investing was attractive*
>
> *8. Only 29% of respondents felt alternative UCITS funds (including absolute return) delivered good outcomes*
>
> *9. In terms of preferred approach, respondents were evenly divided between active, passive, alternative and SmartBETA funds*
>
> *10. In terms of 'useful sources' of fund*

> *information, respondents showed a lack of support for guided fund lists, fund ratings and financial advisors. Instead respondents showed more advocacy for past performance, fees and fund managers themselves.*

The big difficulty is that (as fund selectors) we have not yet fully disentangled the active-passive debate from one of charges and there is little to no universal studies proving the effectiveness of active fund selection among professional buyers. Without a clear message to investors, fund selectors should expect growing individualism, media influence and fund flow herding. This itself presents a very big risk to the fund management industry, which I will explore in the next chapter. More bluntly, if fund selectors continue to allocate assets into the most obvious and popular funds then they are simply sealing their own redundancies. Target acquired. Quod erat demonstrandum.

*#gamifucation*

*Pic. Paternoster Square by St Paul's*

## CHAPTER 10 ▮ CLOWN THINKING AND INVESTOR HERDING

*When Individualism and Media threaten Markets*

I am perturbed (more than the norm). I am on my way to one of my favourite places to stay in London, Pepys Street. I like the Sky Lounge there. Being Northern import scum I hadn't appreciated that Pepys (was actual Samuel Peeps) and insisted on calling it phonetically for the first year ('Pepis', which oft sounds like penis with a Scottish accent) much to the confusion of many a black cabbie. My then colleague corrected me eventually. Once the cabbie had blamed the one-way system sufficiently to excuse the frankly mystical Hackney route chosen, I pass over the customary Scottish 'ten bob note' which is broadly of exchangeable value to Her Majesty's tenner (Ayrton Senna, Paul McKenna etc). This is not why I am perturbed on this occasion. I am on foot from Old Broad to the hotel via St Mary's Axe and Fenchurch, headphones on and listening to my default soundtrack of working in London between 2013-2014 (Oddissee: 'People Hear What They See'). No, on this occasion I perturbed as I am reminded of my old fund flow research upon Thomson Reuters launching a media activity module for their Ikon tool. I also perturbed that id fund selectors are making bad choices; what then of investors? Questions. Does money drives markets; drive money? Does the power of herding have the power to create asset bubbles? Does Efficient Market Hypothesis (EMH) exist, does the media pull the strings, can we break the code of investor risk aversion or indeed conclude that one doesn't exist? An honest account of a simple fund analyst, left with unanswered questions in the wake of 2008.

> *Look no further than the meltdown of the global economy to see an epic paradigmatic failure. Things were just too complex, connected and interrelated, crises proceeds paradigmatic shift. John Marke, 2009, 'Complex Adaptive Systems & Resilience', 2009*

I find human group behaviour fascinating, I am reminded of it every morning in the lanes of queuing traffic on the daily commute. Two lanes of traffic, you move from one lane to the other, trying to predict which lane will move faster with varying degrees of success. It is a capricious and often futile act. Luck has much to do with it but so does herding. 'Is that a heavy vehicle in the left lane?' 'What if the lights are out?' Everyone responds to the flow of traffic individually, they receive similar but slightly different information, at different times, depending where on the road they are. More often they act as a herd. A push and pull effect of lane-jumpers, ditherers, lane stalwarts, lane-timers, the texters, the risk takers, the nervous drivers, the bikes cutting up the middle and the incognisant ('the defaulters'). So to is the push-pull of bullish and bearish behaviour.

That Minsky moment asset bubbles? I can't exactly

remember the origin of my working title 'Clown Thinking', a sort of weak play on 'Cloud Thinking' I suspect. From 2003 I had been monitoring market movements for Franklins. I started researching fund herding patterns back in 2007 and with the help of a digital colleague (the great thinking Mahyad Gilani) we created a tool that actually tracked fund herding against fund sector risk. Being my impulsive self, in a moment of sheer stupidity, I promptly emailed the EVP of Alternative Strategies. No response. Two weeks later I was taken aside by my Californian-based SVP for 'breaking the chain of command'. What I had done was to dare challenge executive thinking of fund development, to its very core, and make my SVP look like a 'shmuck' in the process. In truth we never saw eye-to-eye anyway, 'oil and water' I used to say and so didn't lose much sleep albeit effectively killed-off my career at Franklins that day. I was made redundant eight months later. Bygones.

Why had we caused such a stir? Simply because there is a very big lie at the heart of the fund industry.It is taboo to even utter it; it can only be spoken in hushed tones down empty corridors, be careful as Big Brother is listening and if ever asked you didn't hear it from me. It's an academic misnomer that has persisted for almost 60 years: Modern Portfolio Theory (MPT) is just that, a theory and worse still it's about as real as the tooth fairy. Minsky knew this.

> *"Most mainstream economists were comfortable in believing that bubbles are highly improbable...*

> *Efficient Market Hypothesis (EMH) which holds that markets always incorporate all available public information ... the value of a security would simply be equal to the present discounted value of its future stream of revenue. Otherwise, an arbitrage opportunity would arise and the price would be pushed back to its true fundamental value. Since the recent rise of behavioural finance theory, the view that asset prices always equal the discounted present value of future streams of revenue has been questioned on both theoretical and empirical grounds ... It is now widely recognised that the power of arbitrage is severely limited in the real world markets." Real-World Economics Review, issue no. 50 'What is Minsky all about, anyway?' *KorkutErtürk and GökcerÖzgür [University of Utah, USA]*

Whether MPT and EMH were real once I don't know, but somehow it convinced enough people to invest money. Why? You may ask - there was cash coming out of the Great Depression and a need to convince middle America to trust Wall Street, again with their savings. The reason given was Efficient Market Hypothesis, that information was 'efficient' and if you didn't have it then you had to trust those that did. Information was power and you either had it or you didn't. Professions grew around the information and pseudo-sciences invested to perpetuate the industry. For a while things ran fine, there was plenty of baby-boomer money sloshing around from the 1980s onwards, money itself controlled by a relatively small number of institutions and pension funds. This prevented any ill-effects from the risks in the system, money was invested slowly, conservatively and followed rules and gentlemanly conduct. Risks remained but they were mostly economic and credit-based, not investor/asset driven. What wasn't appreciated was the rate of growth in technology and retail investing.

What changed was the dawn of 24/7 media. Now investors had access to the information and they started making decisions on their own. The growth over 50 years of the lucrative 'retail' market was about to have some unexpected side-effects.

*Fig. Technology: The Low-Latency Imperative: How Fast is Fast Enough?*

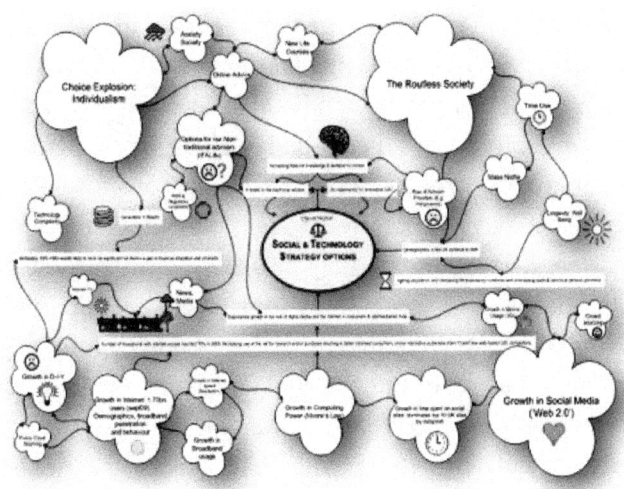

Technological advances move at such a pace, and firms rely on such varying strategies, that the level of latency 'defined as the time it takes for an order to travel to a marketplace and to be executed or cancelled, and then for a confirmation of that activity to return to its source' acceptable to any given party will vary, though none of the intervals are perceptible to the human eye. For the past few years, hardware and software providers have been able to decrease latency exponentially each year. We have gone from talking about milliseconds to microseconds and even nanoseconds.' Daniel Safarik, 'Accelerating Wall Street 2010. Next Stop: Nanoseconds' June 2010, Analytics. InformationWeek.com. Even as far back as 2010, Social Media and Investor Relations showed that the Internet was upon us and rapidly becoming the mainstream media for investment. Source: Darrell Heaps, Q4 Web Systems, April 2010.

Kahnemann/Tversky showed that what actually changes is our perception of a given risk at a given time. What then if we are ill-equipped to handle vast or complex systems of information? I see this as fundamental herding behaviour, running away from one perceived risk towards a lesser or unknown risk. There are of course manipulators, puppet-masters and media who try to use this to their advantage. The problem of over-causation does not lie with the journalist, but with the public. Nobody would pay one dollar to buy a series of abstract statistics reminiscent of a boring college lecture. We want to be told stories, and there is nothing wrong with that, except that we should check more thoroughly whether the story provides consequential distortions of reality. Nassim N. Taleb, The Black Swan, Chapter 6, page 78.

The lab experiments of Kahnemann/Tversky went a long way to expose the irrationality of investors through psychology but what these experiments lack is the social element of investing. To fully appreciate the enormity and complexity of the problem Kahnemann/Tversky would need to re-run a large sample simulation, exposing test subjects to an array of information. Although I doff my hat to psychology to highlight the error in the system, ultimately understanding the problem resides in sociology and behavioural economics. Often the fear of being wrong, for many investors, is stronger than the ambition of being right and beating the market. Many investors overestimate or underestimate their attitude to risk and react differently. This may be because of confusion or distraction; were asked or asked themselves the wrong questions. The problem is that many of those questions are already influenced by a huge array of sources in their daily lives. The investor digital map (below) is a complex adaptive social system:

Markets (and investors) today remain preoccupied about whether they are in a rising or falling market. These markets have become widely known as 'bull' and 'bear' cycles and as high a profile gauge that you will find investors respond to. Traditionally this concept holds we should expect bull markets and at other times bear markets, it's familiar, straightforward and casts the 'bear' as the villain profit-taker and the bull as the hero profit maker. It assumes that risk falls and rises cycle on cycle. Simple. However, what if the level of underlying risk remained constant in the simplest of Newtonian lessons (i.e. it doesn't fall or rise, it simply changes). The 'force' that changes risk is the money flow (asset liquidity) of investors buying and selling as the react to the availability of assets, credit and market information. Market commentators often depict investors as somewhat helpless (hapless) passengers of the market cycle and many investors will feel that to be the case during periods of market turmoil. For many it is easier to think that markets have a life of their own. I propose that only when investors react to information does the market truly react to events.

If I read correctly then Kahnemann/Tversky's analysis into behavioural investing alluded that all types of investor respond to the events around them. If true then their reaction in turn creates risk whether the effect is immediately recognised or not. By building global samples of investor sales flows we can better understand how investors reacted to different situations, the effect on their attitude to risk and how these patterns are changing. It is worth pointing out that professional investors, institutions and traders have the biggest influence on day to day markets. Let's refer to these as intra-cycle movements and they have a large part to play in manipulating markets and economies. They occur from trading behaviours, hedging, asset shifts and holding or investing varying degrees of cash at any one time and would occur even if no money entered or left the industry. This market is very complex and adheres to its own rules and systems. Intra-cycle activities can move the markets relatively easily with small amounts of trading volume. Of course even these investors are subject to the influence of media and their subsequent actions can influence the whole market. What I'm interested i' are the big shifts, the big money movements, the bull/bear markets, the times when investors pick up on big stories and invest/divest accordingly. For now I'll refer to these as extra-cycle movements.

*Fig. Intra versus Extra Cycle Movements'*

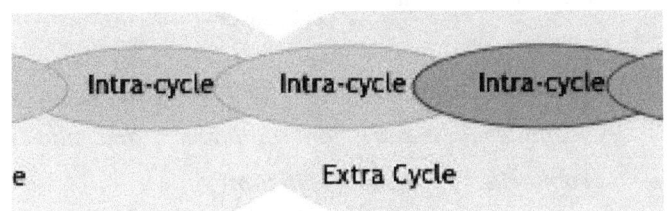

Fidelity's Magellan study back in 2005 showed that investors rarely knew what was good for them. Whereas the Fund was able to average 15% compound annual growth year-on-year; amen, most of its investors rarely bettered 5%. Why? Alas investors chase seem disposed to do exactly what is not good for them ▪ to buy high and sell low. While at my previous fund house I tried to replicate the Magellan study with our own sales data. The only problem with cross-border funds is that everything is traded via omnibus account (i.e. the money is collated through an agent). Tricky! I realised that aggregated flows were sufficient, to a degree, since the Magellan study. Although unable to pinpoint the exact buy and sell points of each investor I could at least hypothesise a range of outcomes. My starting point was an old investor behaviour chart we used at my old firm, itself an expansion of views held by Sir John Templeton, perhaps the original value and contrarian investor, the founder of one of the first global equity funds in 1954. To this I added my own notes, based on a basic assumption that at any given point not all investors are in consensus, there are always two opposing sides, which creates a push-pull effect.

> ▪*"Bull markets are born in pessimism, grow on scepticism, mature on optimism, and die of euphoria." Sir John Templeton*▪

*"Stock markets can be risky and confusing places so investors look to tipsters just as much as punters at the racecourse." David Stamp, 'MarketProphets', page 38, Chapter 2 'Dismal science, dismal record?'*

During my 2008 analysis, whilst at Franklin Templeton, I split flows between BUYs and SELLs across three different time-horizon strategies. Those were (1) short-term 'trading strategies' identified in Fidelity's study, (2) medium-term total return investors and lastly (3) long-term strategic investors. The first group were generally blamed for market volatility, they exacerbated bubbles and drawdowns. By contrast long-term investors were occasionally thanked for helping to counter-balancing volatility. Changes in my investor risk index between 2002 and 2008 identified seven key periods of changing sentiment (herding patterns).

*Fig. 'Investor risk premium scale'*

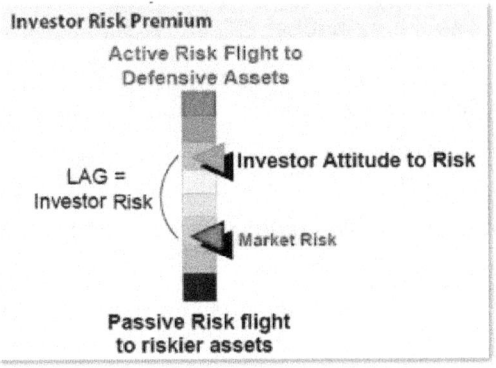

That analysis showed that for any investor buying and selling short-term the rewards were few; longer-term investors fared somewhat better but the compound annual returns were actually strongest over the 1-2 year holding period. The interesting fact for this paper was that buying and selling patterns were not consistent; there was a high degree of shift in sentiment and buying behaviour. These surprising results went against the grain of the conventional view of retail investing. It was further evidence that individualism was growing. The increasingly likely reason should be unsurprising, investors had become more sensitive to market conditions through media influence. Investors are bombarded by an array of information and peer pressure. The angst of the investor is psychological but the problem of investor herding is wholly sociological.

Ernst & Young's UK Item Club, back in 2009, predicted double-digit growth for non-advised investing in 2010. The change is occurring in both retail and corporate, individual contracts and personal accounts will devolve ultimate responsibility away from employers, advisers and trustees to the individual.

Rising markets contain large amounts of 'passive risk', in other words risk that is contained within positive volatility (i.e. profit). Periods of passive risk often corresponded to markets driven by liquidity (increased investing), fuelled by money expansion and/or earnings growth expectations. These are often referred to as 'bull' markets; when driven mostly by liquidity they are sometimes called 'momentum' markets, most recently driven by globalised central bank quantitative easing (QE) from 2009 to 2014. 'Active risk' on the other hand is perhaps best typified by periods of high volatility and/or falling growth, and sometimes referred to as 'bear' or drawdown markets. Active risk is present in any market where high volatility, widening sector ranges and low correlation exists. The last equity bubble correction occurred 2000-2003 after the dot-com crash. In terms of outright volatility and downside then 2007-2009 exhibited active risk on an unprecedented scale.

Perception model: Active risk then is the most measurable and visible form of risk to investors, intermediaries, asset allocators, product managers, sales consultants or marketers. Active risk, itself,is not necessarily the most important risk for future financial planning, asset allocation or product development.

*Fig. 'the traditional pro-cyclical model'*

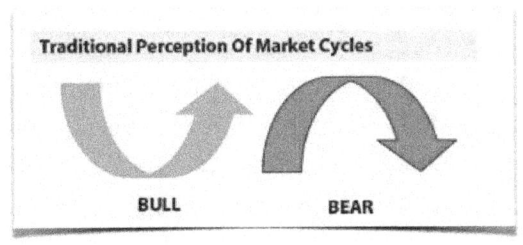

More often risk is confused with downside and similar

regression methods to show variance, loss and negativity. Ex-post recording of physical events such as price drops are different since the risk has already transferred. Stochastic and ex-ante models confuse this simple rule by projecting past/current forward but we all know what Einstein said about math and what David Stamp wrote about forecasting.

*Fig. proposed 'risk-constant perception model'*

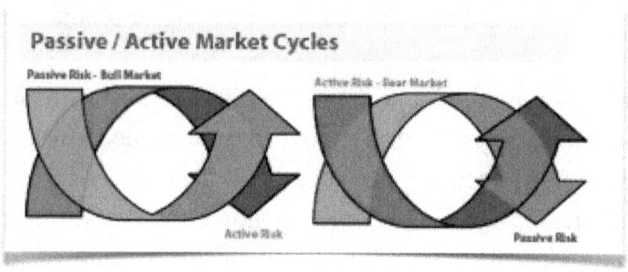

We therefore need to look for risk as yet unnoticed. What most asset allocators still ignore is the risk of media influence. So what is 'media influence'? For years sociologists and media studies academics have strived to work out the effect media has on the individual. Media influence is critical because it is at the beginning and end of the feedback loop of information. It is the alpha and the omega and as such is a deeply conflicted state. Is information itself 'risk'? Risk defines itself only when we try to manage it, box it, control it and otherwise when it makes itself obvious post-event. Most of the time it hides itself in dark corners. It is Media that strives to find Risk, to shine a spotlight on it in order to sell news. 'Risk' has been described to me by peers as the 'expected likelihood of a physical, measurable event yet to happen with no physical manifest. It is the road accident around the next corner, pre-event there is no physical way to measure the cascade of infinite outcomes. Uncertainties then are the risks we simply do not yet know about or have been unable to estimate. Risks in the risk management sense are 'estimates'.

So what then of the media? If risk is contagious, ever present and lacks physical manifest then arguably media is a risk. It is also unique in the way it can both forecast events yet to happen; and manipulate the reporting of events once occurred. Media is also allowed to give superfluous financial advice, cast opinion, over-emphasise events without regulatory recrimination. To this extent the media is akin to a clandestine collective who make money by making news. They are not the friends of the investor nor do they feel regret for stirring up sentiment. Media moguls are the puppet masters of individualism and the most influential and destructive force in the financial industry today. How then do investors react to media? As investors tend to respond to media than actual market movements then this creates a 'lag' effect. This creates the opportunity for under-reaction and over-reaction and can inject further herding risk into the system. We can illustrate the 'lag' between market movement and investor reaction as well as track the effects of investor 'herding' through fund flow data. We can visualise shifting attitudes to risk by illustrating sales patterns into an investor risk premium scale, which very simply weights each sales flow by an assumed level of perceived risk.

Perceived low risk products are positioned at the top of the scale and high risk products at the bottom. In this way volume (liquidity) is very much the driver of the index just as trading volume moves an equity index. The difference here is that only large shifts (across the asset classes) produce discernible results and thus we mitigate asset allocation effect by considering all asset classes at once. The formula is thus simply:

> *The Risk Premium Index is the sum of the Investor Premium Scale (R) multiplied by the net sales flow volume (W) for every discrete monthly observation (t). NB: The index is not cumulative nor takes into account the magnitude of the change relative to residual assets held.*

By tracking changes in the investor risk premium, against sales flows and sector performance, we can spot opportunities for asset allocators, more easily explain diversification to clients, identify new sector opportunities for product development and fund stories for Sales and Marketing. Critically for fund selectors, understanding investor redemption risk is key. If sales flow patterns are part of some intricate elastic web that's continually changing due to behaviours, media flow, performance/risk changes ... action, reaction, re-reaction - then I can see why my earlier analyses had been flawed. (1) I wasn't accounting for a dynamic change in perceived riskiness of different assets (a delta scale was needed) and (2) I wasn't considering the presence oft unseen correlations to other factors.

Are sales flows entropic? One of the main causes of entropy in sales flow pattern is the difference between the residual aversion to risk (that is the balance of asset held long-term) versus the change in aversion to risk (or risk premium) month-on-month. If the residual aversion to risk is the first order variable, then the change in risk premium is the second order (delta), and the change in rate of change of risk premium is the third order (gamma). For example, we may observe a large shift of money flow out of Emerging Equities and a simultaneous large in-flow into Bonds. An easy assumption may be to expect that the money flowed from Emerging Equities into Bonds. However, we don't know this to be true, since the outflow from Emerging Equity funds may have been reallocated across a broad spectrum of other sectors and the inflow from bonds may again have come from other sectors. Here the original observation would have been false. Even less predictable are changes of investor premium within multi-asset solutions wherein the investor has effectively delegated their risk premium to a fund manager or product provider. In order to mitigate for the lack of transparency we look at aggregated positions by volume against long-standing positions. Only then, on balance, do we know when a concerted shift from one end of the risk premium scale to the other has occurred. Investors have become increasingly exposed to media. Since originally developing my methodology back in 2008, mobile network data has exploded and now being analysed by the likes of Thomson Reuters. By plotting sales flow behaviours (risk premium) against events, mobile usage and media flow then we could estimate the effect media has on investors, herding and risk back into the financial system. Fund selectors and distributors need to better understand investor herding and the impact of media influence. Regulation such as the Alternative Investment Fund Management Directive (AIFMD) has changed how fund managers perceive investor and redemption risk, as part of their liquidity risk management. Since the financial crisis we have seen increasing blurring between institutional and retail funds. Consequently analysis has to go beyond simply back-testing the redemption profile of a fund's holders and capture the effects of investor herding and media influence.

Where do I see the cross-over? By plotting sales flow behaviours (risk premium) against events, against mobile usage and news flow we could estimate the effect media has on investors and thus herding and risk levels back into the financial system. Piece by piece we could factor in different elements and begin to measure 'individualism'. Against the backdrop of the fund industry status quo; and the growing individualism among investors, the remainder of this book discusses digitalisation in greater detail and what impact it may have on fund management generally and the fund selector specifically.

*#behaviouraleconomics*


*Fig. Investor Risk Aversion towards Bonds: 2008 Credit Crisis.*

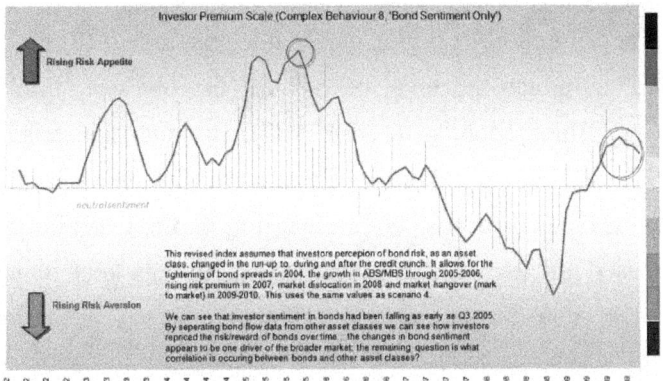

# CHAPTER 11 ■ CHASING THE HOLY GRAIL?

*Why Traditional Quant Analysis is not the Solution*

This is an unashamedly short chapter. I have deep respect for those who are able to apply mathematics into real world problems; I just no longer feel fund management is a problem that can be rationally solved with numbers. Often in the Old Broad office, we would have enjoyable and colourful debates about quantitative and qualitative analysis. The level of affinity to the schools of thought often typify the approach of a fund analyst. We seem to spend a lot of time labelling each other for no discernible reason. As fund analysts we are often derided as the 'blunt end of the stick' of our industry, when it comes to the tricky numbers. We are expected to follow, not challenge. In the last decade we have seen an explosion in actuarial models to calculate the risk of financial instruments. Two things are true of these advances in financial analysis: (1) they became more complex and mathematical and (2) they failed to reduce the level of risk for the investor: think LTCM, Black Monday (19/10/1987), Barings-Asia crisis (1997), dot-com (2000) and the credit crunch (2008). Flash crashes, taper tantrums. We are verging into new territory, increased uncoupling of macro and asset markets. One issue is that the many models retain the same core components: historical price movements and volatility. Most assume that assets will revert to a long-term trend.

Geometric Brownian Motion ('GBM') assumes a strong tendency to trend, it says that returns won't jump from day one to day two but move up and down in fairly predictable increments, the returns of the previous days have an impact on the subsequent day, they are not unique. This estimation of how prices move is the underlying principal for the future pricing of derivatives contracts such as options e.g. to buy a contract, at one price, to then buy or sell the underlying asset at a future date at a future price. This is usually referred to as the 'Black-Scholes formula'. It is often generically described as the old-age 'law of big numbers' (or law of averages) where returns follow a pattern around a mean and that the volatility around that mean diminishes over time. Where those returns are then assumed to form a normal distribution (or bell curve) then the GBM is symmetrical to the mean of those returns. Frankly none of these models have proven particularly reliable or the holy grail hoped for.

Nicholas Taleb dismisses such assumptions, instead he refers to Poincaré's 'scattering' in his book The Black Swan. Running with that model in terms of complex media influence, consider: three interconnected events, with at least two independent variables, each cog moving independently, continually rotating; e.g. this could represent the sales flows of two different sectors following three media events. This is complex; this is adaptive, and it is most certainly not traditional quant.

I shouldn't be so dismissive of quant of course and a clear distinction should be made between actuarial science, behavioural and economic-based models. Perhaps I have a deep-rooted insecurity around Calculus. The appeal of a quantitative or programmable algorithmic approach is that it can be digitalised. I am therefore bound to consider alternative solutions like Pure Group's macroeconomic model or factor attribution suppliers such as Style Research.

*#randomwalk*

*Pic. Apple store,*
*5th Avenue,*
*New York*

# CHAPTER 12 ▪ DIGITALISATION IN FUND MANAGEMENT

*Is Today's Value Chain an Apple Watch away?*

It is purely coincidental that my recent digitalisation article for Portfolio Adviser was entitled 'Rise of the Robots'. Indeed that has been that publication's editor's working title for all things digital and RoboAdvice for some time. The coincidence arises because it was my namesake Bernard Beckett (no known relation) who wrote 'Genesis' in 2006, a philosophical science fiction novel about artificial intelligence and what separates humans from machines. Indeed it was also Samuel Beckett (also no known family connection) who wrote previously about a post-apocalyptic 'Cyborg'.

Consider if the fund management industry, and investors, cannot overcome human biases. Should we seek to supplant them? Can we digitalise them away? Put that question on hold for a moment. Did I ever mention I love mechanical wristwatches and classic cars? I covet their old world engineering despite the presence of more efficient, effective and modern substitutes. The advent of the Apple Watch is a good example. In all unemotional ways it is superior to my ageing Swiss autos, yet I choose to don the inferior choice: is that vanity, prestige, stubbornness, nostalgia or fear? As I watched the launch Apple event I sensed that change 'cometh the hour'. Now no more automatics; just an Apple Watch.

Putting Apple and Google aside, 'digitalisation' i.e. the rise in financial technology ('fintech'). We have entered the age of BIG DATA and one thing big data does is it collates and removes traditional information advantages and creates new data advantages. Today's investment industry is being challenged to update itself into the digital world. Digital does not respect geographic borders, a Californian based digital provider can access clients in Asia and vice versa. Ask, what part of the value chain cannot now be digitalised?

Nutmeg: One of the largest disrupters in the market since the launch of Hargreaves Lansdown's Vantage platform, led by Nick Hungerford, Nutmeg is one of the liveliest B2C and retail centric offerings. Nick describes Nutmeg as 'the UK's first online discretionary investment management company.' The proposition entices investors to 'Get an intelligent, fully-managed portfolio'. Based on customer information, Nutmeg digitally builds and manages a portfolio by 'diversifying your investments to avoid putting all your eggs in one basket'. Nutmeg monitors each portfolio, adjusting the asset allocation appropriately and rebalancing every month, at no extra cost. Nutmeg aims to do this low cost accords and according to each customer risk rating. On visiting the site you are initially confronted by the bright hues of green, white and orange and a large login prompt, initially off-putting you quickly realise you can navigate to other parts of the site to learn more. Nutmeg have links to see the past performance of the ten portfolios and the overall feel is one of ease of use and transparency, upfront fees, key people, debunked of jargon and unashamedly devoid of the 'personal' aspects of traditional wealth management. This is an uncluttered website, backed up with video links and an ever so cute 'nutmegonomics' blog. This is the model many are attracted to and others hope to imitate.

WealthHorizon: Led by Chris Williams, Bristol-based Wealth Horizon typifies the post-Hargreaves digital SME appearing around the country and clustering in the Bristol area. The firm describes itself as having grown out of a 'realisation that the traditional advice and investment management models are not serving the majority of people in this country.' WealthHorizon's messaging is increasingly familiar: digital, low cost, passive. WealthHorizon attempts to bridge the gap between digital non-advice propositions and traditional wealth management. It proposes an escape for disillusioned masses away from the active fund marketing machine of the industry. The service is online, with optional access to human advisers, and offering risk-adjusted portfolios (supported by Parmenion) employing underlying passive investments. First impressions are good with a clean colourful looking home page. Investors get a fully-tailored risk-adjusted portfolio, all of which WealthHorizon suggests can be completed in under 30 minutes.

> ∎*The simple fact is, buying an active fund is a total lottery, with one year's star performer next year's dunce. Investors often hold just a handful of funds in their portfolio which will invariably include some of the biggest and most popular funds but a lot of these will disappoint investors*∎
> *(Chris Williams, WealthHorizon)*

Fundhouse: Established South African based fund rating firebrands, Fundhouse has launched into the UK with a series of punchy fund reports, most notably a negative 'Tier 3' rating of Standard Life's super-tanker GARS fund. Led by Rory Maguire the service issues free one-page rating notes and pay-to-view detailed fund ratings reports. The site focuses on the B2B model and both look and feel is certainty more professional than high street. In reality anyone can register to the website to read the free content. Premium content is only available to FCA registered advisers and fund selectors. The paid subscription service appears to be the core way this model intends to monetise itself short term but I have no doubt the firm will benefit from acquiring a few large contracts to allow expansion and has every chance. The service challenges the fund ratings status quo in a number of ways, firstly it appears to be a non 'pay-to-play' model and by that I mean that the fund manager does not pay in any way for the rating received. The old pay-to-play model had long been criticised by fund buyers and fund managers alike and one factor why the S&P fund ratings business (the then dominant player) was wound up by McGraw-Hill, much to the shock of the City. This model was supplanted by the 'marketing rights' model. In this arrangement the fund managers are invoiced by the agencies for 'marketing rights' to use the fund ratings in their literature, website and fact sheets. Fundhouse do not follow this model and have a clearer user-based model, which in turn fully aligns Fundhouse to the fund buyer rather than the fund manager.

> *As Rory Maguire says 'it's the equivalent of 30 fee-paying advisers, for one fund manager's fees. The raters used to have pay-to-play, now what is written on the invoice to managers is "marketing*

> *rights". Somehow it snuck past the RDR rules, which still surprises me. It's hard to understand how a product provider can directly pay an advice business, thought RDR fixed that.'*

Secondly and perhaps most critically to this question, Fundhouse is prepared to rate a fund manager absent of a face to face meeting, for example in the event the fund manager is unavailable or unwilling to meet. Naturally, by offering candid ratings, this can be a challenge, but fund managers appear accommodative. Fundhouse estimate that 90% of the time they get meetings with the managers only 10% prefer to stay outside Fundhouse's process. The fund manager meeting has been held sacrosanct by qualitative fund analysts. Fund analysts have long held an information advantage over advisers and investors through better face to face access to fund managers. Coupled with that more independent fee model, Fundhouse therefore tests a cornerstone of traditional fund ratings. Given fund managers are increasingly digitalising content online, including fund manager videos, then perhaps Fundhouse has timed the UK market perfectly. Digital services question whether fund analysts still have an information advantage and casts doubt on the value of the fund selector. A raft of punchy ratings will certainly raise some brows. I expect Fundhouse may face resistance from both fund managers, and other fund analysts, if later judged to be effectively masterless rōnin. But the overall approach of Fundhouse has to be applauded, at very least the move away from the pay-to-play model. A subscription approach should endow independence and generate trust among fund buyers.

Pure Group: Pure, both tacit and implicit, is positioned as a B2B solution. Pure Group's mission is to meet the changing landscape of the Investment and Savings industry through a digital service. The initial look and feel of the website is clean, understated, with a black background, upmarket look and screams serious business. Pure Group describes itself as 'an independent company embracing technological and regulatory changes and the impact this is having on the investment and savings industry.' Pure's quant engine is forward-looking and on face value looks innovative, backed by US academics, to generate fund ratings that are linked to performance, correlation and macro assumptions at different points of the market cycle. In essence Pure goes one step further than Fundhouse and fully eschews the manager-analyst experience, which avoids the inherent lag created by the traditional cyclical review process. Pure backs this all up with analytics and statistical software using Cloud technology to speed the flow of information to the investor. What Pure may miss are non-macro and non-performance factors, but then so can the fund analyst. Pure's online blog is comprised of macro charts to further enrich the information to the end user. Overall the proposition is professional and appears well positioned for advisers seeking to improve/modernise their supply chain, digitalise their own offering or reduce the cost of their fund research. What is exciting about Pure is that the different approach may produce less overlap with established rating agencies. In my eyes, the logical conclusion of Pure's mission is arguably D2C via a simplified analytical service.

> *The apparent lack of digital innovation around the fund management industry can partly be explained by the fragmented distribution chain and a concern of the regulatory environment, especially when engaging end customers.We believe this lack of innovation will change with the emergence of new and specialist "FinTech" businesses who will provide tools and services to help asset managers and advisers focus on the needs of their customers. Digitalisation will ultimately help the fund industry improve the overall customer experience and engage with the broader consumer market in Europe who have a low ownership of long term investment products*

> *and secondly, hold more than 40% of household wealth in cash.' (Patrick Murphy, founder PureGroup)*

Fundinfo: fundinfo bills itself as the users' 'source for global fund information' and proposes that sustainable, profitable investments require well informed fund investors. The site offers instant, free access to more than 11 million fund documents, data, videos and ratings from more than 700 fund houses. It does not originate content. The business model appears to be B2B, funded by and working with fund companies to provide a single source of information for fund buyers. It is effectively a digital library, an Amazon marketplace or Kelkoo for fund manager information but without the ability to buy, rate or leave feedback. fundinfo even spells this out on their site:

> *'Fund providers stand to benefit from fundinfo, too: By publishing their documents and distributing them to all users by email, fundinfo saves them a considerable amount of time and money.'*

Fundinfo provides additional enterprise warehouse facilities such as 'paperboy' for the hosting of prospectus, other regulated documents, marketing material and videos.

fundinfo has also worked with fund rating agencies like Fitch. The Fitch rating business is a traditional fund rating proposition. Linking to a more innovative digital partner, like fundinfo, is strategically sound without committing much CapEx. It expands Fitch's coverage and thereby encourages more fund managers to want to market Fitch ratings and, as with most rating agencies, more market coverage means more potential marketing fees. In turn, fundinfo benefits from high quality fund 'IP' that is otherwise difficult for digital providers to originate. Therein fundinfo offers a variety of flavours with similar tie ups with Morningstar, Lipper, Citywire and Sauren offered free of charge to the user. This stands fundinfo apart from both Fundhouse and Pure, philosophically; effectively a new world offering built upon an old world fee model directly charged to fund groups. That said, it does make the best of the available fund ratings today and could benefit further from linking to innovative suppliers like Fundhouse, Square Mile and Pure. Whether too many ratings just become noise is an interesting notion, but far easier to assume buyers like choice and will pick their favourites. Some keen fund buyers may even seek out the overlap and consensus that exists between most agencies. The potential to later monetise fundinfo D2C, through online trading, would seem possible but would require changes to both site layout, origination of unique content, and business model to compete with the very best available today.

What then for the fund investor? Simply that more of the

value chain can now be digitalised. The investor also has more routes to market and has more access to information to base decisions, compare advice received and measure investment outcomes. For example: Investor A feeds into an online 'about you' customer and attitude to survey, they can engage an adviser online, access online asset allocation tools, set their rebalancing and lifestyle preferences, assets are then digitally transferred from the investor's bank account or payroll to the investment account, the investment is digitally invested through program trades into a risk-rated multi-asset fund or basket of ETFs, the investor receives online valuations and portfolio information. The investor subscribes to the Bloomberg app for free, joins some recommended fund investor groups on Facebook and follows known financial commentators on Twitter. The investor later changes their risk preference online, the investor eventually requests to draw down assets online, sells the investment online or transfers to another digital provider. The end.

What then for the financial adviser? Robo-advice versus digitalised human advisers? A prominent but, as yet, unresolved, debate is whether standardised robotic solutions can replace more holistic advisers and wealth planning. Client trust can take many forms: it can be the trust formed from simplicity, transparency, accessibility and value for money or trust built around softer factors such as diligence, holistic assessments, bespoke tailoring, reliability and the fiduciary bond. Whatever factors traditional advisers cite, they will need to qualify and evidence those virtues and benefits more readily in future. Robo-advice will compete with more traditional services in the cloud, with cost, accessibility, transparency and functionality all key. Meanwhile traditional advisers have been dogged in the past by mis-selling reviews, adapting to the Retail Distribution Review and the stigma left behind by the commission model. Advisers in aggregate also do not have a good track record at investing assets or picking funds (if contemporary research is to be believed). Establishing a clear brand, skills, values and customer experience will be essential for the traditional adviser while building a clear digital presence with strong functionality both pre and post advice. Likewise digital propositions cannot fall back on the human interaction and will live or die by the investor's experience of their first visit to their website and repeat visits thereafter. Digital platforms must also ensure that form does not overtake the function of delivering suitable advice. This debate is set to run and run.

What then for the fund selector? While developments of digitalisation could be a real threat for traditional fund research; adopting technology now may actually prove the selector's greatest ally. After all the Cloud promises fast accessible information about fund managers and a means to communicate views back to investors and make timely asset allocation calls. Take the Due Diligence Questionnaire for example. The Due Diligence Questionnaire (DDQ), otherwise often known as the Request for Proposal (RFP) or Request for Information

(RFI) document has long challenged the fund selector community and fund managers alike. The issue arises in the uniqueness of each individual questionnaire. Commonality and duplication is masked by different terminology, wording and bespoke criteria. Increasing regulation in the fund space, like EMIR, MIFID, AIFMD, has ballooned DDQ requirements and fund selectors find themselves increasingly under pressure from Risk colleagues and Audit to demonstrate effective due diligence was performed? Despite this being the 'digital age', the DDQ process hasn't changed significantly in a decade despite huge advancements in fund complexity and regulation. Groups like fundinfo are gradually adding more and more DDQ information to their website.

What then for the fund manager? Consider that even investments like Exchange Traded Funds (ETF) represent a new digital open-ended, exchange-traded investment and continue to gain greater market share every day. They are not a physical asset, they are electronically traded, backed by either a basket of stocks, reference index or synthetic instruments. They are priced, valued, traded and viewed entirely in the Cloud. Meanwhile traditional collectives, with their slower settlement periods, are gradually reforming, which begs a question. Is the purported 'zero sum game' among active funds due to outmoded methods of transmission? Asset managers have responded by increasing the size of their RFP teams to accommodate and we have often seen RFP teams well in excess of 20 people. Ultimately that growing operational cost is passed back to investors at some point, which during a cycle of fee margin compression and austerity will become increasingly unpopular. The creation of digitalised fund information in the Cloud (like fundinfo) may ultimately help both fund manager and fund selector alike.

What then for the mid and back office supplier? Another area to be put under the spotlight is the additional expenses ('back office') that arise from fund management. My expectation is that fee compression will inevitably have an impact right along the value chain and services with fixed fees will face the risk of digital substitutes. Where global service providers have effectively operated in the past as near-cartels yet fund managers, previously content with plenty of margin to go around, will now be left with no choice but to bring in-house or seek lower cost solutions. In my paper 'Oligopoly Orchestration' I alluded that scale asset managers were now running ever larger fund books, leveraging internal back offices to maintain flat operating costs or outsource to large back office suppliers and enjoy fee ladders with the rising AUM. Therefore the scope to do new fund deals with capped or even zero additional expenses is here. However, lower scale boutiques will struggle to match these super-tankers, as services such as transfer agency, brokerage, research, audit, fund accounting, custody tend to have fixed or floating pricing per AUM. This may move more boutiques towards multi-boutique platforms like BNY. When it comes to suppliers, boutiques tend to be price-takers but my hope is that they find innovative low-cost digital substitutes. New funds are disadvantaged at outset due to proportionally high fixed costs that gradually reduce as assets grow. This model clearly incentivises the promotion and buying of larger funds and needs to change. External suppliers will therefore have to respond and redesign their service to be more flexible and become more 'capital-lite'. That leaves marketing and distribution costs and we have already seen how distributors and platforms like Nutmeg are finding new innovative ways to lower those costs. Again the solution is in the Cloud, fee compression and Digitalisation that will reach far back into the fund and platform supply chain. Discretionary fund managers and fund selectors still have a window of opportunity to become or engage digital platforms, to use technology to become more efficient and thereby refocus their economic value. Advisers can refocus their efforts around understanding the investor journey, tax and family planning. The value chain as a whole is realigning and that chain will be digital in the future. I invite other fund selectors, platforms, discretionary fund managers, Cloud suppliers and advisers to a symposium to create an innovative digital think-tank. It will be an opportunity to discuss new synergies and map what the future of the fund value chain could look like over the next decade. Moreover this is an opportunity for a more democratic and transparent industry, one that delivers a better economic value to the end investor and more evenly divided earnings through the chain? Self-learning AI algorithms are set to be disruptive. Advice, Allocation Information, Selection, Valuation, Maturity. Obsoletion or Cyborg, you choose? *#fintech*

## CHAPTER 13 ▪ ETF INNOVATION v ACTIVE MANAGEMENT

*When will we see the Tesla of the Fund Market?*

I had just finished a product trial and it had changed my perceptions of what a digital can achieve. Thinking about digitalisation existentially in a broad industry context is one thing and inevitable but can its impact be much more direct? Can digitalisation really reach into the very heart of active fund management? The Exchange Traded Fund (ETF) celebrated 20 years since State Street first listed its SPDR fund. Different fund groups are now developing an ever-diverse universe of ETF strategies. These pose a very direct competition to traditional active mutual funds. What products like ETFs are doing is shortening the trading time from market to investor and from investor back into the market. Of course this may have positive consequences, such as introducing a faster pressure release for negative news, reduction of 'lag effect', less build-up and less overreaction. Most ETFs also promise some degree of WYSIWYG transparency and lower trading costs, they are generally seen as a good deal for the individual investor. Potentially ETFs may make investors victims of their success because products like ETFs may introduce new forms of herding risk. Recently I was prompted to revaluate my biases when I encountered the Tesla electric car.

Prologue: The electric car is a far older invention than

people realise and in fact would have probably gone onto become the dominant form of automotive propulsion if not for the intervention of oil company cartels and car manufacturers. The electric car has been in development for over 100 years albeit the last 20 years has seen accelerated advancements. Similarly over the last 20 years we have seen the gradual development of Exchange Traded Funds (ETFs). Both enjoying a Moore-like tailwind. Like Autos, ETFs have been resisted by the incumbent industry. As a blue collared fund analyst, I don't have a strong academic background per se (undergraduate degree and a back catalogue of level 3 and 4 professional qualifications) and there are only really two subjects I know much about, investment funds and cars. Unsurprisingly, my love of cars pre-dates that of my interest of fund strategy, our reading room is an orchestra of cookery books, travel, biographic, economic and fiction (my wife Jenny's) and a smaller collection of automotive and investment (my books). Between us, Jenny is most certainly the reader and educated. My own collection includes a full set of the industry 'design yearbook', marque-specific books, racing books, generic books, historical books. I am an even bigger car geek than a fund one, as hard as that is to believe. That love of cars took me to a test drive of one of the most controversial cars available today, a digital disrupter of the premium establishment. Tesla.

My Tesla P85S test drive, March 2015.Tesla Motors was

formed in July 2003 by Martin Eberhard and Marc Tarpenning, who financed the company prior to Elon Musk's involvement. Musk joined Tesla's Board of Directors as its Chairman in 2004. Tesla's primary goal was to commercialise electric vehicles, starting with a premium sports car then moving into more mainstream vehicles, including sedans and affordable compacts. Test driving the Tesla was a revelation. It is a big car yet the design is sporty, with good lines, has good visibility and is an easy car to place on the road, progress is swift and effortless. Like Nikolai Tesla himself, the car is revolutionary, electric based but more importantly a digital disrupter of the traditional mould. The session was relaxed and personal, quickly getting to the car, orientation and out onto the road. Under the watchful guise of Steve Edge, Tesla's test drive sales representative, we discussed the Tesla's dynamics, styling, product and price positioning, Daimler Benz, performance, materials. Steve probably wasn't expecting 20 questions but the discussion was very amicable and soon the test drive was over. Saying the Tesla is an extremely easy car to drive, is an understatement, it is beautifully made like no other car I have sat in and the technology is truly game changing and will appeal greatly to the smartphone and tablet generation. Unlike any other test drive I have taken there was no hard sell, which only warms you to the car even more. Other manufacturers should take note.

Conscience but no soul? One inescapable fact for the motoring enthusiast is that it is often a car's imperfections which create a sense of identity and convey an existential 'self' beyond metal, leather and plastic. For many, myself included, the engine defines a car's heart, a string that the Tesla cannot pull on. Its identity is unashamedly modern despite some styling nods to the status quo and an attempt to appear conventionally handsome with recognisable language in common to Lexus, Maserati, Jaguar XJ and Aston Martin albeit significantly cheaper Mondeo and larger Hyundai models are probably a bit irksome for Tesla's design studio, given the P85 is a £60-70k premium saloon (née sedan). The Tesla therefore defines itself by its prominent technology, whisper electric drive, ability to update firmware, superior materials, sense of serenity, but minus that combustion personality. That is probably going to be the tough bit for the would-be buyer to get their head around, filled with 100 years of motoring nostalgia. Similarly it took drivers about 10 years to fully warm to diesel-powered cars ('oil burners') which also lack a pleasing soundtrack.

In comparison then the character of the Tesla far is less emotional than my classic or the wife's older 911 but significantly more pleasing than the agricultural tones of our diesel 4x4. Given existing buyers of executive diesels have already eschewed charismatic petrol engines then they should be an easy crowd to win over. The one aspect Tesla will need to address is the range of a Tesla versus the uberAutobahn marathon mile chomping diesels which can now reach 600-800 miles in one tank. What will help has been the trend growth in diesel prices over the last decade as demand for diesel-rocketed and continues to carry a healthy premium over petrol, at the pump, even if global oil prices have fallen. As Tesla is now pushing beyond 400 miles of low cost commuting then diesel buyers should become increasingly attracted, especially with the launch of the Tesla 3, Tesla X SUV and if Tesla can bring the entry level P85 into the sub-50k bracket. Meanwhile it's highly possible that the emotive commodity of 'character' will eventually become swept away by the appetite for technology. How many of us truly covet a keyboard, Acorn Electron or calculator? A nice Mont Blanc or Cross pen perhaps but again the trend is shifting as a generation of fund buyers retire to give way to a new generation of tech-savvy, pen-shy buyers. I am somewhere in the middle but I was an early adopter of the iPad at launch. I recall in fund meetings and workshops that I was often the only one to be using a tablet. Occasionally some would use a laptop but most deferred to pen and paper. Now I observe that up to half of attendees are using tablets of some manufacture, fund managers are using tablets and often they are used instead of paper documents or to allow interactive elements during a presentation or conference. I am now on my third iPad iteration.

**Lessons for the Fund Industry?** Is there anything remotely that we can learn for wealth and fund management? Tesla sees itself as a technology company, not a car-maker. I have yet to hear a fund manager say the same thing to me but I suspect it will come. Like automotive, the wealth and fund value chain is also facing digital disrupters like Nick Hungerford's Nutmeg, which in many aspects shares a DNA with Tesla and in a similar way has put incumbent players on the back foot. The notion of a 'soulless' investment should be considered when designing SmartBETA products. For example if an investor wants the investment to support Corporate, Ethical or Social Governance ('CESG') then these considerations need to be factored into the specification at outset or by the index provider. By comparison an active manager can evolve to these changing demands. Likewise if an investor wants to support decarbonisation and sustainable investing then these also need to be specified at outset. On the other hand an index-based product should (on paper at least) be less susceptible to fraud, corruption or negligence.

Passive and factor investing funds are devoid of personality and that offers the fund selector little information advantage and unsurprisingly many fund selectors are resistant. Consequently passive providers have increasingly targeted D2C distribution channels. Some fund selectors have created active-passive propositions, which apply an active asset allocation atop a basket of passive funds. Passives are often an easy fix to the lower the 'double-tap' cost of a high fee fund of funds. Like the Tesla, fund investment should be about the most efficient means to extract performance for the lowest cost. Yet the last 20 years indicates fund selectors have not always done the best job of choosing the most effective funds. The Local Government Pension Scheme (LGPS) report by Hymans Robertson in December 2013 and the running 10-year study by S&P Dow Jones (SPIVA) indicate that active managers have under-performed passives more often than not. This is not to say active managers 'never out-perform', they do, but they tend to revert to mean due to style bias and the changing market cycle. However, through reinvestment, even with that mean reversion, good active managers can still prove superior over the longer term. The debate is what constitutes a reasonable holding with which to compare to and does not factor in effective fund manager selection. Many studies call into question the value of active fund managers. Most tend to be compiled by non-fund buyers and rely on large aggregated samples and thus miss what is on the ground. Take the LGPS report by Hymans Robertson in 2013. The first thing to note about the study was that the terms of reference was to 'find savings', most likely from reducing exposure to higher charging fund managers. The second was the authors were not fund buyers. Therefore some implied bias was set at outset to favour lower cost funds and rely heavily on aggregate quantitative data. As just about every fund manager I know has a unique time horizon then aggregation studies will inevitably revert to mean and indicate at least half of managers are under-performing. How much more than median gives some indication to the quality of fund selection and ongoing due diligence (or lack of).

On reading this actuarial super-tanker paper, of some displacement, its conclusions appear to infer poor legacy fund selection decisions by LGPS, as well as a great number of unanswered questions around alternative funds. The overall tone was that LGPS was paying too much for older actively managed funds, which were underperforming benchmarks. Professional fund selectors will rightly point out that scheme trustees are usually laypeople and lack formal training or experience in fund management. The LGPS is perhaps then not the best proxy of the merits of active management and selection. What it does well is send a very large message to the market that many legacy active funds may be similarly lagging benchmarks and charging for the privilege. What it also indicated (to me) was that it was very easy to pick average or below average active managers and most professional fund buyers would agree on this point. In my 2013 paper 'Key Man Risk Misnomer', I challenged established conventions around how fund selectors choose fund managers and the rise of star fund manager culture over the last 20 years. Choosing funds on fund manager personality or gravitas is a moot point within the industry. There is a growing cognisance that marketing by the larger houses and investment media has created a star manager culture that simply does not stack up on less emotional measures.

Electric Evolution? Introduced 20 years ago by State Street the SPDR Exchange Traded Fund was the first to market but like electric cars did not represent the ultimate evolution. Much like today's hybrid electric-powered cars, the current crop of ETFs are probably a mid-evolution towards a more developed technology somewhere off in the next decade. In truth, active fund managers, wealth managers and distributors have a lot to still address regarding the technology within their firms and along the supply chain to digitalise, make more efficient and lower cost. Digitalisation goes way beyond a slick website and my forthcoming papers will tackle the specific challenges. Only once front, mid and back offices have been digitalised and aligned will active management be ready to fully commute into ETFs, traded electronically and settled within 'T+1'. What could a fund game changer look like?

- *SmartBETA fund with multi factor investing, e.g. IShares, SPDR, JP Morgan*
- *Absolute Return ETFs, e.g. Goldman Sachs GCRTX, IndexIQ, GURU, Powershares Multi Strategy Alternative, Julex*
- *Long short equity ETFs, e.g. AdvisorShares, FirstTrust*
- *Volatility ETFs, e.g. HVPW Put Write*

*Index fund*

- *Arbitrage ETFs, e.g. Proshares MRGR*
- *Active ETFs, e.g. JP Morgan, AdvisorShares*
- *Quant strategy ETFs, e.g. QuantShares, Credit Suisse, AdvisorShares*

*"Asset managers are now competing on their operating capabilities, what they used to think of as 'the back office' has become a critical factor in their business success."* Stephen G. Meyer, Executive Vice President of SEI

Fifty Shades of Active? The Tesla shows that even a car can become a digital product. So must actively managed investment funds if they are to compete with the growing innovation among ETFs. In time ETFs may even become the default method of investment transmission for all funds. Compared to electric vehicles, ETFs have only been in development for one-fifth of the time and are even less constrained by the physical world. Thus current ETF solutions remain 'hybrids', a prelude and not the final evolution. Like Tesla, innovative ETF providers would do well to review their fees to drive home an advantage. What then hampers rapid development of actively managed funds are archaic trading, regulation and fund management systems. This opens the door for attuned fund managers who are prepared to invest into digitalised business models. This goes way beyond a website, digital 'app' or social media presence. Cynical pro-passive commentators like blogger 'The Investor' in an article entitled 'Weekend reading: ETFs are playing to the active crowd' are right to question the value of all of these new strategies coming to market, but there's the rub. Are ETFs, as the article quotes Bogle, the 'gateway drug into active investing'? We can address efficiency of transmission and cost but active strategies still need to deliver and require more expertise to appraise. To do that we at least need to unbundle the cost from the active-passive debate. Once we do then there is a chance that long-term studies like S&P Dow would begin to evolve from black/white to shades of grey (hopefully not fifty). If active management is to survive then it will at least need to address cost as a very minimum. I invite fund managers to engage with distributors and fund buyers to consider both digital barriers and solutions. What the investment equivalent of Tesla will look like makes for an electrifying discussion. *#teslafund*

*Pic. Shot from the driver seat of the Tesla P85*

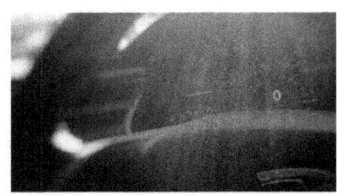

## CHAPTER 14 ▌ A DIGITAL DEATH?

*Can Asset Management Adapt to Digitalisation?*

Death? Question mark. As I sit between fund meetings in Moorgate and Gresham, arguably I have saved the most contentious topic to last. Thinking back to what I wrote in earlier chapters, can fund selectors themselves survive the move to digitalisation? Possibly. Can the value of fund selectors be digitalised? Probably. Currently the fund industry faces many dysfunctions, between selectors and fund managers, and fund managers, distributors and investors. In the first chapter I discussed the search for optimum alignment, part of which is digitalisation. To have a place in the future value chain, fund selectors need to employ digitalisation better. A key factor touched on before in this book is the concept of information advantage and how fund selectors choose to interact with fund managers tomorrow. For example the Due Diligence Questionnaire (DDQ), otherwise often known as the Request for Proposal (RFP) or Request for Information (RFI) document has long challenged the fund selector community and fund managers alike. The issue arises in the uniqueness of each individual questionnaire. Commonality and duplication is masked by different terminology, wording and bespoke criteria. Despite this being the 'digital age', the DDQ process hasn't changed significantly in a decade despite huge advancements in fund complexity and regulation. The modern world is moving fast and time is becoming an increasingly precious commodity. The current DDQ approach produces time and cost for fund selectors and managers alike.

As a big fan of cars and motorsport I was saddened to see the demise of some of the smaller teams in F1. Alan Tovey wrote in The Times (1 November 2014) about the demise of Caterham F1 and that 'the bill for designing and building 200mph cars, maintaining them and paying their drivers and staff, along with transporting the whole circus to 19 races across the world is reported to run to $120m (£75m) a year 'and that's just the price of keeping a mid-tier team racing.' As with running a F1 team, running an asset firm is an expensive business and, like F1, firms go to the wall. Like F1 there is a sense of survival of the fittest in asset management and a general agnosticism about small groups struggling. However, all firms are feeling the pinch between rising regulatory and operational costs and falling revenue margins. Boutiques and larger firms alike could therefore benefit from more efficient ways of working, as could fund selectors.

The problem? Expansion of the fund selection sector and improvement in investment education has driven ever more complex requirements. Fund strategies themselves have become casino complex with the advent of 'Alternative UCITS' funds. Ultimately this all increases the cost and time required in an exponential fashion. Asset managers also supply their own 'standard' document but the reality is that no two houses are alike and this can increase the time it takes the fund selectors to analyse and compare submissions from multiple managers. Often fund selectors are not prepared (or able) to only accept the fund manager's document. Increasing regulation in the fund space, like EMIR, MIFID, AIFMD, has ballooned DDQ requirements and fund selectors find themselves increasingly under pressure from Risk colleagues and Audit to demonstrate effective due diligence was performed. By contrast the average investor; while not able to access all available information due to MIFID, has no compliance requirements in how they use information and document their decisions. Digitalisation has narrowed the information gap; regulation has widened the compliance burden. Asset managers have responded by increasing the size of their RFP teams to accommodate and we have often seen RFP teams in excess of 20 people. Ultimately that growing operational cost is passed back to investors at some point, which during a cycle of fee margin compression and austerity will become increasingly unpopular. RFP requests tend to generate a lot of secondary inefficiency within an asset firm because of the way that requests are often channelled (e.g. through Sales). The urgency created around the opportunity to tender often draws in many more people than simply the RFP team: Fund managers, marketing, product development managers, compliance, risk team and on and on. The burden on boutique firms is particularly onerous and we believe standardisation of some of the DDQ process will help alleviate resource pressures on smaller firms and benefit long-term competition with large asset managers.

That 80:20 rule: Standardising the DDQ creates efficiencies for both selectors and fund houses. Many fund selectors document a proprietary process to their fund selection and the DDQ is often related to this but what if we standardised 80% of the common requirements of most fund selectors, allowing fund selectors more time to focus in on their 20% add-value? A good question. The main stumbling block thus far appears to be the fund selectors themselves, a sense of paranoia to not give up 'trade secrets'. My old colleague taught me much about the workings of the industry; I can still hear his words now echoing in my ears: 'loose lips, sink ships JB'. Most fund manager RFP teams will tell you that there is actually very little unique content from one RFP to the next, but different formatting is a challenge. If you think you currently have an information edge over everyone else, most likely you don't. Ultimately if fund selectors do not find better ways to collate fund information then they risk becoming redundant, cut out by online tools, advisers and investors.

Another way fund analysts can use the 'Cloud' is to become a proper network. At the moment you have somewhere in the region of 5000 analysts running around in silos, seeing managers, scrutinising RFPs, studying portfolios, running performance reports, completing attribution analysis and writing opinion. What I am not talking about here is the increase in fund research delegation, which has been the trend over the last few years. Instead I am talking about fund analysts working as a crowd, feeding research from local managers into a global network. If you are thinking this all sounds a bit communist cum hippy commune then you may be right but I see the great strides being made in the Crowd Funding space and cannot help but wonder that a better way is possible through digitalisation, to achieve optimum alignment among fund analysts and investors. Cutting their carbon footprint along the way. Having originally written New Fund Order I was proud to become an ambassador for the Transparency Task Force in 2016. Transparency (as much as fintech) must be at the heart of the new fund order in order to rebuild investor trust, alignment and optimum economic value.

*#TransparencyTF*

*Pic. St Olave's, Pepys Street nr Tower Hill and Fenchurch*

## CHAPTER 15 ▮ REVELATIONS

*Loose Lips Sink Ships?*

If you can recognise and accept that our industry has been a fairly insular and incestuous one; then we are part way to a solution. The awkward truth for Digital is that much on the 'Net' is ugly, trivial and far from educational. So too is the awkward truth for fund selection, in porn-parlance, there is no quick 'happy ending'. It is tempting to ignore all this digital hooey given that ballooning mutual fund assets has made the last few years a very lucrative one for many. While fund selection practices have largely remained unchanged for a decade; the technological world has turned on its axis. The commodity of information has changed due to Digitalisation and with it the information-advantage of the fund research industry. It can be best summed up easily by an acronym I came across recently 'LMGTFY' (Let Me Google That For You). With some base understanding any investor can become a proficient fund selector. Many in the industry will refuse to recognise these issues. I don't intend to be pious in my observations. God knows I have made enough mistakes and trodden enough grey areas in my time. This is also not a confessional, and not my Catholic guilt creeping through.

Many of my peers may dislike my sharing some insider taboos, which I appreciate but can live with. Having written this book, an unfair accusation that might be levied is one of 'sour grapes'. That as a perennial under-achiever I am somehow, effectively, scuttling my own ship, betraying my own kind. Bollocks. Instead I am trying to tackle issues that are doing a good job of killing our profession quietly and gradually, with the hope of finding a solution. I used to be an overly modest young man but soon realised that modesty is just a quick way to being overlooked. Thankfully my wife Jenny, friends and family are there to keep me on terra firma for I do not seek to operate in ivory towers but rather than coffee shops of Old Street. If then I can leave some sort of indelible mark on a field I have pursued for nigh on two decades then good. If I can help effect change and align fund selection for the betterment of investors then even better. Lastly, if I can be part of the fintech revolution then I will feel at least to have been relevant to the modern age.

The bad news for fund selectors is that I don't pretend to have all the answers but I am left full of questions. Questions that few in my field are prepared to openly discuss. Fund selectors and multi-managers have enjoyed 20 years of working without challenge, safe within an information advantage bubble, over advisers and the man (and woman) on the street. Pressure on active management and the exponential expansion of the Internet endangers this status quo. Of the current 5000 UK fund analysts today (guesstimate) I expect 10-20% at best will survive the next decade. For many, multi-managers will be consolidated and ultimately merged into lower cost multi-asset propositions. The closure of the S&P fund ratings business in 2013 was publicly a shock to most in the fund research fraternity but privately many saw it coming. Secretly most felt that their 'pay-to-play' model was always doomed and that S&P had struggled to adapt. Thankfully most of my friends found new homes but it was a telling moment. New research firms like Square Mile, led by Rich Romer-Lee, have partially helped to fill the void but I feel that sensation of a rollercoaster just as it gets to the top, before the Big Dipper (I'll caveat that I hate rollercoasters and even struggle on a Wurlitzer). That feeling of lost control, the process of fund delegation changing, the business of fund selection becoming commoditised as the profession itself contracts. Funds of active funds are already on borrowed time, their double-tap charges will lead to a 'Tom Clancy' double-tap to the head and cannot be saved. 'Tango down'!

Survival guide. Professional fund buyers should quickly pause to consider:

> *1.     Changes to the value chain, a question of alignment*
> 
> *2.     Growing investor individualism, herding and the role of media*
> 
> *3.     Investment and due diligence of super-tanker funds*
> 
> *4.     The need for better fund governance, look beneath the bonnet*
> 
> *5.     Challenging those star fund manager biases*
> 
> *6.     Preserving healthy competition between fund groups, avoiding oligopolies*
> 
> *7.     Making use of increasing innovation in Exchange Traded Funds (ETFs)*
> 
> *8.     Best approach to selecting absolute return and long-short funds*
> 
> *9.     Reviewing 'safe' fund choices and core-satellite approaches*
> 
> *10.    Using digital to improve the DDQ process and streamline research*

RIP? As I sit here writing this in the metropolis that is

Islington (just off Angel station) dark clouds hover above as, I ponder the future. My bandwidth (in all senses of the word) is at best mid strength. I wash the blood off my gloves. We can all see that the fund industry is undergoing great change. Traditional multi-manager, as it has existed for decades, will die to be replaced by multi-asset. Darwin might say that if fund selectors are to survive change then they will have to adapt, to re-evaluate how they align themselves to investors, products, fund managers, addressing old biases and embracing digitalisation (now). If we want our legacy to be greater than a drawer full of branded pens, USB sticks and moleskin writing pads then I encourage my colleagues and those in the fund industry to come together to discuss the challenges and opportunities emerging from this new fund order. Likewise should any fintech start-ups or enlightened wealth or asset managers seek an increasingly redundant fund selector then please tweet, poke or otherwise link-me. For now, only one flight home beckons, two hours to get to Bank, £10 left on the Oyster card, catch the DLR from platform 9, back to City for the ten past four, then home. One armoured flight case, check. Tango down, check. 47. Numbers.

*#newfundorder*

*Pic. The trusty flight case*

## CHAPTER 16 ▪ RESURRECTION 2.0

*Surviving the New Fund Order in 2016 and Beyond?*

12 months pass quickly, time to regroup. 2.0 is an update not a rewrite. However since first writing 'New Fund Order (1.0)' I have had many interesting conversations with other fund buyers, speaking opportunities, fintech start-ups, think tanks, media engagements and meetings with asset managers. It has shown me that the industry is finally willing to explore new options, begrudgingly perhaps but with more consensus that the status quo is on borrowed time. Since writing NFO.1.0 we have also had the WikiLeaks Panama Papers scandal, which felt like a final nail in the offshore wealth coffin. Fintech looms over the City like a 200 foot Godzilla, waiting for investors to reject current value chains. Fintechs are ready to fill the gaps and obsolete as much of asset management as it can. The transparency and cost agenda has stepped up a gear and passives are outselling active funds at an increasingly alarming multiple. Professional fund buyers are no longer oblivious to the fact and ready to embrace technology to improve their economic value, lower costs and remove unnecessary middlemen. Hospitality is being scrutinised more than ever before, events less flashy. Version 2.0 then affords me the chance to not only correct a few bugs in 1.0 but also update the book to reflect the last 12 months and offer some solutions. Take boutiques for example..

In November 2015 I wrote a paper entitled: 'The Seed, the Crowd and the Deep Boutique Sea'. Since the Retail Distribution Review (RDR), boutiques have come under increasing competitive and regulatory pressure in the UK market. Boutiques struggle to attract long term institutional buyers and thus a) struggle to build AUM and b) suffer volatile short-term AUM. Boutiques also suffer economies of scale and less able to discount fees compared to larger asset firms. This section examines the relevant issues and proposes a new solution based on experience from crowd-funding. It is hard to not be impressed by the dynamism of the crowd funding sector. It looks so easy and so devoid of the onerous regulation that we face in our industry. Under the veneer, today's asset management is inflexible and deeply divisive towards innovation. Instead the industry has become commoditised, large asset firms have become M&A companies in a similar way to how large Pharmas used to buy-up small Biotechs, or Tech giants in the social media space, to access patents and new revenue streams. That's a big problem for fund buyers, future alpha discovery and return on investor capital.

**Background**

Regulation has significantly constricted larger institutional buyers and distributors from seeding smaller asset managers, which we can broadly refer to as 'boutiques' or otherwise 'specialist' asset managers. However it doesn't have to be thus. The opportunity for innovative Third Party Marketers ('TPMs') partnering with compelling boutique managers, matching fund buyers within a transparent digital cross-border service, is exciting.

There are a lot of semantics around what constitutes a 'boutique', the traditional definition of 'offering a narrow fund line-up' clearly becomes a mockery when firms like Artemis can manage AUM at significant multiples to the average small firm. For clarity let's define a boutique as any small asset firm, struggling in the lower deciles of the IA size rankings. Consultants Sheffield Haworth defined it as follows:
- A specialist approach to investing, for example focusing on a certain sector or serving a particular type of client.
- A smaller presence both in AUM and headcount than global asset management houses.
- Part or sole ownership by the investment team, as opposed to being owned by private investors

Five key issues have exacerbated this divisive conundrum:
1. PRA regulation and Solvency 2 is dissuading insurers from creating reinsurance agreements and segregated mandates, which used to be near level playing fields for small and large asset managers,
2. Post MIFID regulation, AIFMD and FACTA has pinched the sale of offshore non-UCITS into the UK (UCIS, QIFs, LLPs etc),
3. Mimic buying behaviour, fund selection delegation and general concentration of buy ideas and assets, fuelled in part by star manager culture and marketing dominance of larger IA firms, *#ratingtheraters*
4. UCITS and COLL rule restrictions in terms of maximum fund holding, plus additional bank rules around shareholder exposure (minority interest),
5. Merger and Acquisition (M&A) activity by both large asset firms (Schroder, Standard Life) and super multi-boutique firms, e.g. BNY, Natixis and Legg Mason, *#oligopolyorchestration*

Furthermore an issue that needs to be considered before any form of crowd funding or syndication can be employed is antitrust and competition law. Lastly we also need to deal with the taboo for institutional fund buyers, dilutions and swing pricing.

> *"Boutique fund managers face difficulty in raising assets for a number of reasons.. boutiques cannot be as competitive with fees, distribution budgets are being cut and.. an inability to receive allocations from long-term institutional investors due to capacity constraints means that many boutiques are suffering from having a large percentage of short-term investors. This is damaging to their AUM as these investors will often redeem at the first sign of economic difficulty." Sheffield Haworth.*

**Why choose a boutique?**

Day to day I observe that boutique managers more often operate like private equity managers, they buy companies not stocks, they finance businesses where they see growth, they have higher active share, they hold smaller capitalisation stocks, they hold for longer and they are less likely to buy the familiar stocks held by everyone else. Many boutique managers are self-invested and owners of their own businesses, which in turn builds alignment between investor and fund manager. Unfortunately few advisers and investors recognise the merits of such an approach, many prefer well known managers and confuse unfamiliarity with risk and visa versa.

Over the last two decades the asset industry has undergone radical change. Significant growth in global AUM has allowed the market to be able to support more participants. Consultants Sheffield Haworth noted:

- *"The growing desire amongst top performers at large asset managers to have more control over their investments has inspired them to join boutiques where they have the freedom to do this.*
- *Regulations such as the Dodd-Frank Act prompted a mini boom, as traders have spun out of banks.*
- *The widely held view that large asset managers have become too big to be profitable and that increased bureaucracy has impacted performance levels, creating a space in the market for performance chasing boutiques.*
- *Perhaps most interestingly, there has been a growing sophistication in the investor base in recent decades which has created the demand for boutiques to launch with esoteric business models."*

According to crowdsourcing.org global crowdfunding experienced accelerated growth in 2014, expanding by 167 percent to reach $16.2 billion raised, up from $6.1 billion in 2013. In 2015, the industry is set to more than double once again, on its way to raising $34.4 billion. These figures are based on Massolution's 2015CF – Crowdfunding Industry Report. The Massolution research team collected information on 1250 active crowdfunding platforms (CFPs) across the world, including high-quality data submitted by 463 CFPs to the Crowdfunding Industry Survey, before undertaking significant further research and analysis in order to reach its results. What can fund buyers and marketers learn? Crowd-thinking.

**The Hedge Fund and Private Market Experience:** Institutional Pensions Europe reported in 2012 how the asset manager Hermes (wholly owned by the BT pension) provides boutiques with accelerator capital, in partnership with Northern Life. This entailed locking seed money for three years, then withdrawing initial capital but providing further capital for a further four years, as the boutiques reach critical mass. Meanwhile innovative hedge seeding providers like IMQ through its IMQubator service had been drawing praise in the hedge world. *"The plan is to provide acceleration capital to smaller managers, those with track records of two to three years and already have some AuM; less than EUR100m for example,"* Jeroen Tielman, IMQ founder. With this new platform, IMQ will position itself as the "developer and manager" of a portfolio of hedge fund strategies, in the form of managed accounts, and in doing so providing a strategic partner with the advantages of outsourcing and insourcing whilst eliminating the disadvantages.

Meanwhile Markus Hill wrote *'Real Assets and Funds Boutiques – Seed Money and German "Middle Class Thinking"'* in 2011. *""Small" companies in the real asset area are beginning to break new ground in regard to the feedback given by institutional investors. Projects often develop along process lines – project sketch, feedback from specialists and potential investors, optimisation and then, in the most favourable case, inclusion in the investment program – long processes which from an economic point of view (diffusion of new process and product knowledge) have to be shortened. In the conception, the providers can "sharpen their axes" in the sense of effecting thorough preliminary work in advance of the conception.*

*In front of the background of low interest rates certain investors might be able to exhibit increased business acumen and widen their own investment horizon. The dialogue with the "small project initiator" could become more intensive as is the case today with the dialogue between funds boutiques. Barriers in which openings must made with great involvement by both sides!"*

The business model for seed investors has proven lucrative on the hedge fund industry, based on analysis by Larch Lane *'Hedge Fund Seeding: A Compelling Alternative'.* "Seeders benefit as well. Providing early capital typically entitles seeders (both direct seeders and investors in seeding vehicles) to share in the hedge fund's revenue ("enhanced economics"). This participation can be quite profitable and takes a number of different forms, which we discuss below (see "Enhanced Economics of Hedge Fund Seeding"). Seeders can also gain other advantages such as early exposure to emerging managers, rights to future capacity, seeding rights for future funds, full transparency, risk controls and the potential right to monetise their profit participation at a future date." Exploring (albeit more regulated) economic models for mainstream boutiques might similarly benefit seed investors over the long term, providing a tangible premium to offset exposure in early years.

### The Challenges for Small Funds
*Regulation, MIFID and MIFID2:* Exactly what is in MiFID2 is something of a moot point, as there has been a delay to the issuance of technical standards. The key challenge (besides additional compliance) is the expected impact on broker research and access arrangements.

These effectively allow smaller firms to expand their research in exchange for dealing commissions through brokerages. Smaller asset managers who do not have the scale for internal research functions may see their research ability cut and left with difficult choices around how to resource. NCI and Open Europe's research has concluded that: *"An outright ban on the cost of research being passed on to investors would clearly favour larger asset management companies – especially those that can afford their own in-house research services."* The New City Initiative and Open Europe published a paper in June 2015 entitled *'Asset management in Europe: The case for reform'*

> *"The investment management community and especially the 'boutique' (i.e. smaller firms) community find that the regulatory burden imposed upon them by the EU (AIFMD, MiFID II, etc.) is so expensive and onerous, that in themselves these regulations are an issue in terms of our business sector prospering.. At a time when Europe is struggling to find its way back to economic growth, it becomes all the more important to safeguard a sound and vibrant asset management industry."* Dominic Johnson, Chairman of New City Initiative.

*Core-Satellite Conundrum:* In my earlier chapter I suggested that fund buyers were at risk of *game theory* in making 'safe' choices around well known funds. In my 2014 paper *'QED: Active versus Passive'* I noted that the problem is undoubtedly the result of past imbalances in marketing spend, broker commission and distribution reach of the largest houses versus boutiques.

These create perceptual context (or relative gaming) problems for the fund buyer. Firstly it can skew value for money if say a large group of sector funds are more expensive that would otherwise be justifiable. Secondly boutique funds may simply present less attractively to a buyer used to a well know name and accompanying marketing machine. The other problem is that the narrative of 'success' has centred around chasing tail performance and related fund awards. The implication is that poor fund selection practices among advisers and flows to popular retail funds may have skewed the 'average' performance of active funds.

*Concentration Rules:* Various rules can restrict how much institutional investors can hold in an individual fund. For example UCITS limit investment to a maximum of 25% of the units of the underlying fund. Many buyers struggle to buy funds below £100m and satisfy their own compliance requirements.

*Merger & Acquisitions:* An increasing number of boutiques are being bought out by larger asset managers. I debated in my 2014 paper 'Oligopoly Orchestration' that this activity is ultimately damaging for long term competition, performance survivorship bias and for fund buyers. WSJ reported in July 2015 that

"According to the study by State Street, investment firms class acquisitions as the top source of opportunity – ahead of the likes of entering new markets and expanding distribution. State Street surveyed 400 senior asset management professionals across 23 countries." and that "According to asset management M&A advisory firm Pakenham Partners, there were 121 M&A deals globally in 2014 involving asset management businesses with assets of more than $500 million."

"While this was fewer than the 150 deals in 2013, the size of deals has risen. The disclosed M&A deal value hit $17.1 billion in 2014, compared with $13.7 billion in 2013, and the assets transacted reached $1.81 trillion, their highest level since 2009. Some 95% said they see "positive scope" for acquisitions, significantly up on the 74.5% recorded last year. Indeed, some 46% said they are currently weighing up acquisition openings, which State Street described as "one sign of the momentous changes" impacting the fund management industry." The risk to boutiques is clear, being driven to the surface by regulatory an market pressures into the jaws of awaiting M&A predators. As more and more institutional buyers turn away from boutiques, it is no wonder that small firms might find the only offer on the table to be a buy-out.

*Competition Law:* Expanding the AUM available to boutiques is ultimately good for the long-term competition of the asset management industry. However EU competition law (antitrust law in the US) has a fundamental bearing on the prospects for boutiques and somewhat ironically must be traversed with care to make this a reality. In its September 2015 paper, in collaboration with the Competition Markets Authority, entitled 'Competition law and wholesale markets' the FCA notes:

*"There are three broad types of anti-competitive behaviour, discussed in further detail below:*
*i. Cartels;*
*ii. Other anti-competitive agreements or concerted practices; and*
*iii. Abuse of dominant market position."*

Clearly the key creation of a crowd-funding or syndication to support boutiques could be misconstrued as a 'cartel'. The paper is clear to note the penalties of cartel behaviour *"Cartel behaviour can have the most detrimental impact on competition, which is why engaging in cartel activity may lead to criminal prosecution of individuals (under the cartel offence in the Enterprise Act 2002), as well as fines imposed on firms (under UK/EU legislation on anti- competitive agreements and arrangements)."* Therefore it is crucial to address the distinctions for the proposed model.

**Cartels:** What is a cartel according to FCA/CMA? *"Cartels are a serious form of anti-competitive behaviour and involve two or more competitor firms agreeing, whether formally or informally, to limit or cease competition between them. The operation of a cartel may involve price-fixing, market sharing, bid-rigging, limiting the supply or production of goods or services, or information exchange. The agreement or arrangement between competitors could be formed in many ways — including a written contract, a conversation over the phone or at a social event, a meeting or chat room, or via emails."*

By contrast the proposed syndicate model would involve concurrently multiple potential buyers, the boutique manager and the third party marketer. The differentiators to a cartel being: 1) the syndicate is managed by the TPM for the benefit of the boutique manager, 2) the buyers are not in direct competition with each other for the purposes of raising seed capital, 3) information shared is to aid transparency and fairness between all parties including 4) a single price shared across the syndicate enabling 5) a group of buyers to engage with a single supplier and to reiterate 6) access to the boutique is not exclusive nor restricted at any point.

The interests and actions of all parties are formally set out from outset and the purpose of the syndicate is to access seeding capital that would be otherwise unavailable. However should any of the buyer parties meet privately without the boutique or TPM then this could stray into the cartel definition. The paper provides 3 key examples of cartel behaviour, none of which contravene the proposed model:

- *Price-fixing: agreeing with one or more competitors (directly or indirectly) the prices at which to supply products or services to clients (such prices could include commissions, fees, interest rates, benchmark submissions, discounts or rebates).*
- *Market sharing: agreeing with one or more competitors to share customers or markets. Examples include where firms: agree among themselves not to compete in providing certain financial instruments or services; agree not to compete with one another in certain territories; or agree not to compete with one another for certain classes of customer.*
- *Agreeing to limit production or sales:*
- *Engaging in bid-rigging: where a group of firms agree to collaborate over their response to a competitive auction or tender; for example by agreeing not to undercut each other on price or to 'take turns' and rotate the order among them.*
- *Other anti-competitive agreements or concerted practices\**

\*For clarity the TPM would approach the FCA to confirm that the proposed model would not construe 'concerted practices' in context to anti-competition rules.

**Vertical agreements:** If we agree that the proposed model does not construe a cartel, then does it fall under any other type of anti-competitive arrangement? The paper proposes the following tests for a 'vertical' arrangement:

- *Direct or indirect communication of non-public commercially sensitive information such as future pricing intentions between competitors.*
- *Agreements between a firm and its client which restrict the price and/or terms on which that client can resell a product, service, instrument or data. For example, a firm may require a client not to sell products below a certain price or impose a condition that the client cannot resell a financial instrument to the firm's competitors.*
- *Where a group of firms (or individuals within such firms) work together to prevent other competitors from entering the market, thus protecting their position in the market. For example, by imposing criteria or fees for participating in a market that discriminate against smaller players or new entrants in a way that is not objectively justifiable.*
- *Where a group of firms (or individuals within such firms) agree to work together to prohibit the development or introduction of new technologies which could reduce their influence in the market and/or reduce their profits.*
- *Where a group of firms agree to work primarily or exclusively with another firm(s) in a related (upstream or downstream) market, and in exchange get beneficial terms placing them at a competitive advantage to their rivals. For example where a group of asset management firms enter into an agreement with an investment bank in return for beneficial treatment.* *

**\*All of the above examples would not apply to the proposed model.** However the last point is one that needs careful consideration. Currently preferential *'early bird'* terms are common place within the fund industry on a single buyer-to-fund basis. Extending terms to a group of buyers does not prima facie appear less competitive. If such practices were restricted (e.g. MiFID2) then there will be a levelling of the playing field to the extent the syndicate would simply initiate at the lowest publicly quoted price, assuming the size of the book build meets the minimum investment threshold.

Moreover the proposed model is designed to allow more widespread investment into boutiques and thereby improve the long term competition of the fund management industry. The FCA states the sort of agreements that will be exempt: *"Not all such agreements will breach the law. An agreement or arrangement will be 'exempt' from the UK or EU law on anti-competitive agreements and arrangements if (broadly speaking) it brings economic or technical benefits which are passed on to consumers and is restrictive of competition only to the extent absolutely necessary (ie is 'indispensable') to achieving those benefits. For example, some exclusivity agreements will be exempt if they bring a new product to market, provided that the exclusivity lasts only for a limited period necessary to achieve that."*

Taking the above into consideration, in my opinion the proposed model does not appear to fall into the definitions of anti-competitive agreements, as defined by the FCA and CMA.

> 'the proposed model does not fall into the definitions of anti-competitive agreements, as defined by the FCA and CMA.'

*Redemptions and Dilutions:* Sheffield Haworth noted

> *"Boutiques often struggle with redemptions in their early years and many close as a consequence. One way to get around this and to ensure that the business has the capital to grow would be to introduce different fees for different levels of liquidity, thus enticing investors to accept liquidity restrictions in exchange for reduced fees."*

*Star Manager Culture:* Sheffield Haworth also noted *"many boutiques have been taken over by larger managers since the onset of the financial crisis, one of the major facilitating factors behind these transactions has been an inability of the smaller houses to market themselves (due to the lack of a brand name)."* In my 2013 paper *'Key Man Misnomer'* I noted that for well over a decade we fund selectors had become obsessed about fund managers, to characterise them, to invest on the strength of what they say, what they do, who they are. This obsession has been fuelled by the mighty marketing machines of the fund houses and media. Then when managers leave, it becomes the biggest news of the day. In many instances these biases should be challenged. *#keymanmisnomer*

*Costs:* Sheffield Haworth again noted "Boutique fund managers are facing increased financial pressures from industry regulations which larger managers are better financially equipped to handle, for example the costs of bringing on internal or external consultants for risk or compliance reasons. In these turbulent times, cost management is proving difficult for boutiques. Many are suffering from the consequences of being run by fund managers rather than business managers."

*Fees:* Sheffield Haworth lastly noted "Boutiques need to be more competitive with fees from day one, in order to compete with larger managers. One way to attract investors would be to reduce management fees; this could be paid for by raising performance fees. Since boutiques need strong performance in early years to survive anyway, this would be a logical step."

*Location:* Asset managers have traditionally dominated key London locations to be near to fund buyers. However consultants Sheffield Haworth note "Post crisis, financial centres no longer dominate; boutiques are regularly being set up outside of London, and this is seen by many investors as a positive. Businesses based outside London are now recognised as upholding a sensible work-life balance for their employees."

Sheffield Haworth noted "Although acquiring seeding from a larger firm was previously seen as a negative for a new asset manager, it is now seen by many as a lucrative stamp of approval. If a boutique business is struggling after the first couple of years, 'accelerator capital' is a way for them to acquire a capital injection without having to give up as much control of the business as they would have with initial seeding." Again a crowd approach to seeding may help provide a more diversified and stable asset base.

*"boutiques are still the investment vehicle of choice for performance hungry investors and fund of funds whose mandate is to discover under the radar top performing boutiques."*
*Sheffield Haworth*

## *Syndicated-Seeding*: A Crowd-Boutique Proposal

Taking into account the above, and assuming the compliance minefield can be traversed, then I propose a new crowd-based seeding model. This model will serve boutique managers seeking critical mass, and fund buyers looking to increase their ability to buy earlier into new manager stories. The main stages of a crowd approach being:

1. *Research buyer needs:* Engage and network with a range of institutional, private bank and family office buyers to target sectors and ongoing searches. Ideally that network should extend beyond multiple locations and buyer type,

2. *Research available Boutiques in target sectors:* This process will include searching the market sad travelling to meet new Boutiques,

3. *On-boarding new Boutique:* This process is designed to ensure the Boutique is fit for purpose and offers a compelling proposition for prospective buyers. The selection process mirrors that employed by multi-managers and institutional buyers. Data collated helps populate the RFP and concludes with entering into a TPM contract with the Boutique,

4. *Request for Proposal:* The TPM supports the Boutique with due diligence requests from fund buyers ahead of the book build phase. The RFP may include a digital 'beauty parade' between Boutique and buyers (e.g. BrightTalk). If positive responses are received, from a sufficient number of institutional buyers, then the TPM initiates a book build. The fee of the TPM is disclosed to buyers during the RFP as is the target assets/buyers and target capacity for the Boutique. The Boutique delegates to the TPM to negotiate agreed pricing,

5. *Book build phase:* This may last anywhere up to 6 months and can be complimented alongside the RFP and due diligence process of the institutional buyers. The book build facilitates the size of initial assets required to be raised (say 250m) and corresponding number of institutional buyers (e.g. 5x50m). Book building is common place in the private banking market and the time allowable actually compliments the slower buying behaviour of institutional buyers,

6. *Confirmation of book build completion:* The TPM notifies the Boutique, and all interested buyers, that sufficient assets have been raised and details of settlement. If insufficient assets have been raised then the TPM will engage both Boutiques and buyers as to: a) extend the book build period, b) proceed to settlement or c) postpone the book build,

7. *Confirmation/Settlement:* All buyers open accounts and send transfer amounts to the Boutique, traded through CREST, SWIFT etc. Confirmation is also sent out to the TPM,

8. *Post-settlement support:* This may include ongoing Boutique marketing and support of buyer queries following the initial exercise to raise assets. These services are agreed at outset between Boutique and TPM in the TPM agreement,

9. *Redemptions:* Upon an institutional instructing a large redemption then the Boutique will typically reserve the right to apply a dilution levy. The levy protects both the Boutique, the fund NAV and interests of existing fund holders. Alternatively if the selling buyer delays or staggers the redemption then the TPM/Boutique can decide to go to the other holders to raise offsetting assets (like a capital call) or initiate a new book build to identify new buyers. With offsetting flows the Boutique may be able to absorb the redemption without applying a dilution levy for the benefit of all parties.

10. *Monitoring:* Any outcomes arising from the monitoring of one member of the crowd group can be shared with other members, which will maximise resources, aid transparency and limit surprises. Monitoring can be supported with digital update conferences.

**The Solution:**
Of course any Third Party Marketer comes with an associated cost, which will be in the typical range of 15-40bps and thus presents a cost to the Boutique against the Annual Management Charge ('AMC'). That said, it is a cost only against assets gathered, thus a drag in terms of uplifted earnings and also a deferred cost versus investing greater fixed costs in an in-house distribution. It is a question of opportunity cost versus resources and reach. Factor in that, as distribution costs have fallen post Retail Distribution Review (RDR), then so to do boutiques have greater capacity to enlist multiple TPMs. TPMs offer a variable cost, rather than expanding in their own Distribution that presents am ongoing cost irrespective of assets gathered. As to whether to invest in conventional Distribution or TPM, the cross-over fund-to-fund will vary but tends to occur around £500m to £1bn AUM. That said as the pressures of fee compression continue then boutiques may do well to invest in scalable TPMs over fixed cost conventional Distribution.

**The next question for a boutique is of course, which TPM?**
Traditionally selecting a TPM was based primarily around a firm's ability to market and distribute to a broad network of potential buyers, or to market into markets beyond the reach of the boutique's own sales (i.e. outside London).

However the new crowd-funding model centres around matching boutiques to the needs of smaller groups of institutional and family office buyers. This changes the TPMs core discipline from one of outright sales, to one of the ability to select the right boutiques for the right buyers and to more accurately target buyer needs in advance. This in turn requires more technical knowledge to select and on-board the right boutiques and to empathise and understand fund buyer requirements. In other words boutiques should look for different skills in their TPM. Many existing TPMs lack the technical and fund-buyer background to identify the right Boutiques and match buyer needs. It is no surprise that we are seeing more fund buyers becoming TPMs to manage the changing dynamics of the market.

## What are the advantages of a crowd-funded TPM for professional fund buyers?

- Initial due diligence and selection, by the TPM, enhances the fund buyer's own research. In the Funds Brands 'FB50' 2015 report, the top boutique brand attributes as ranked by professional fund buyers were:
- Solidity,
- Appealing investment strategy,
- Stability of investment management team,
- Experts in what they do.
- First-mover advantage and Alpha discovery sooner in the lifecycle of an asset manager

*"Specialist boutiques, with their distinct product propositions, are in a much stronger position to attract business than medium-sized managers operating in the middle ground. Often, they have a more interesting story to recount to potential clients, with their founders and passion for investment bestowing distinct personality on their brands. And while high-conviction specialists will not become the mainstream norm, recent market volatility has highlighted the downside of opting for passive investment, as investors are dragged down in tandem. Low-cost options can come at a price!" FundBuyer Focus 2015*

- The benefit of peer analysis and due-diligence during the book-build phase,
- Ability to invest larger sums, into smaller funds, without increased holdings exposure,
- No additional costs, TPM fee is built into the Boutique's AMC,
- Transparent pricing for both Boutique and buyers,
- Boutique premium? Contemporary studies support that fund managers tend to outperform when managing smaller assets

*"AMG, which invests in an affiliate network of firms which are themselves boutiques, says that the average boutique outperformed the average non-boutique in nine of 11 equity product categories over the past 20 years by an average annual 51 basis points."*

**What next?** Small is beautiful certainly but all boutiques, I know, would welcome being just that little bigger. Improving sales into boutiques will help ease industry asset concentration and M&A activity in recent years. I invite regulators, fund buyers and boutiques to reach out to engage collectively and discuss with me the viability of this model. The opportunities for both boutiques and buyers, through a new breed of third party marketers, look overwhelmingly positive. *#crowdseeding*

### Fintech Reinventing Fund Ratings?

What about fund ratings? Well, consider how digitalisation has entered so much of our daily lives. Imagine if we could explain it to ourselves from twenty years ago. Meanwhile an increasing wave of broad studies have challenged the very foundation of our ability to select funds and pick winners. The battle lines have been drawn between active and passive fund management; with costs and SmartBETA as antagonists in the mix. So far this year (2016) I have already, quietly, assessed around 100 fund managers. Most involved on-site visits, beauty parades, due diligence questionnaires and various analysis. It entails a lot of countless hours of work but to what end? There is nothing quite like getting up each morning, as a professional fund buyer, to read media that questions my very worth. Unless you manage a fund of fund, is there a way to help capture that ability as a fund buyer? The fund rating and consulting landscape has changed in recent years, with established agencies exiting to be replaced by new firms, gradual proliferation and blurring of lines between agencies (like Morningstar), multi-managers (like Russells) and DC consultants (like Mercers).

I see a range of ratings reliance among fund buyers, from those wholly dependent on rating advocacy, to agencies being gatekeepers and influencing platform buy lists, growing presence within fund databases and media, a support tool to validate a proprietary view, right through to being utterly ignored. Part of the issue is that advisers find it hard to ascertain the relative merit of rating agencies or understand their business models.

Therefore a huge opportunity exists to demonstrate economic value through fund selection. To achieve this means working with rather than against fintechs, as the wider RoboAdvice debate seems to be heading. Uploading analyst views into a common platform would allow investors track analyst performance. There is onus too on rating agencies and DC consultants to ensure their ratings are as reliable on the day of the trade as they were on the day the rating first went live. I suggest they too could load their ratings onto a common platform. Lastly annual fund awards could be uploaded and similarly scrutinised. All data used should be time-stamped and ratings monitored on an ongoing basis, with transparent performance shown since the rating was first applied.

New start-ups like Tel-Aviv based SharingAlpha.com show the way and should be applauded. The era of Fintech fund ratings may be here.

*"Our vision is to offer the investment community a better way to select winning funds and at the same time to offer fund selectors the option of building their own proven long term track record. It's about time that funds will be ranked on the basis of parameters that have been proven to work and Fund Selectors will be judged on their ability to add value to investors"* says co-founder Oren Kaplan.

## Alt' Liquids - Addressing Complexity

Until fairly recently (say 2015) and ignoring Brexit - Diversified Growth Fund ('DGF') managers had a fair amount of hubris it was fair to say. Life was good, book builds burgeoning and returns and flows were positive. More recent times have been more testing albeit this has yet to translate into a sales slowdown. It is a useful time then to take stock, debunk why DGF funds are popular and what they offer. DGFs are sold on their go-anywhere ability, to navigate varying terrain just like Sports Utility Vehicles (SUVs) from modest urban jungle to the odd bit of grass, gravel and snow. They are a cross-over product of daily traded retail fund and hedge-like strategies.

One can extrapolate the rise of new products from the needs that bely them. Some products defy current needs by redefining new lifestyles like Smart phones. Take Sport or Small Utility Vehicles (or SUVs), did their exponential rise result as an increased need for outdoor pursuits? Unlikely. No then have come to dominate our roads, somewhat surprisingly, because of a desire for the following:

- *Safety, modern SUVs tend to score highest on passenger protection, particularly little Timmy and Jemimah in the back on the school run,*
- *Celebrity endorsement through the Wife and Girlfriends of football players ('WAGs'), that helped give rise to the 'Chelsea Tractor' phenomenon,*
- *The growth of sleeping policemen ('speed bumps') which the modern SUV can tackle with aplomb. Such road impediments tend to herd around schools, positive correlation one muses,*

- *Climatic change has seen a general rise in four wheel drive, austerity and over population has seen a deterioration in road quality,*
- *Proliferation of urbanisation away from city centres has led to more people commute by road over longer distances, we also often spend more time stationary than moving,*
- *The expanding waistlines of occupants including child obesity, little Timmy and Jemimah ain't so little anymore, due in part of being limo'd a half mile to school watching all forms of multimedia instead of just using the leg stumps adorned in designer stamped sweatshop merch,*
- *Slick marketing that still conjure aspirational notions of outdoor pursuits (that few users will actually practice).*

*Sales* flows globally have risen sharply for SUV (otherwise known as cross-overs). Global penetration is up as reported by IGS Global Insight. With an increase of 13% to 1.2m sales, the mid-sized crossover segment in Europe has grown for the sixth consecutive year, almost doubling its volume since 2009. In the US, Small utility vehicles are now selling at five times the rate they did in 2000. The US auto industry reported that 34% of all new vehicles sold were SUVs and cross-overs. Bear in mind as backdrop how many pick-ups are also sold in the US. These small SUVs are selling at a pace of nearly 20 percent growth per month while demand for small and mid-size sedans is falling. We have seen similar trends in Asia and other markets. A tempting analogy to make might be if SUVs are akin to DGFs then conventional compacts and sedans resemble traditional long only equity and bond funds. The rise in SUV sales is also great news for Automakers because SUVs can be charged at a premium to traditional products. A marketing dream.

So to are Diversified Growth Funds. Diversified Growth and Absolute Return funds (Alternative Liquid) can also be thought of as daily traded UCITS compliant hedge funds. They are a little like the SUVs of the asset world. They sort of resemble the original off-roader (hedge fund) but have been softened for the retail market and more accessible. Like hedge funds, the sales of large off-roaders are in demise. Originally designed for one purpose, DGFs are now used for a seemingly endless range of reasons. They are the quintessential lifestyle investment product, what they should do is provide some degree of volatility dampening. They are rarely tailored and pool investors together within an explicit or implicit risk budget. Many of these strategies have spawned income variants to service the growing income drawdown market in the UK and beyond. Initially highly concentrated around a few supertanker funds; since 2008 the sector has become much more proliferated with an ever bewildering range of options. It has become the prized 'me too' product for asset CEOs and the 'game in town' for Distribution.

Likewise sales flows into DGF funds have risen dramatically. Like SUVs there appears to be a large lifestyle element in favour of DGFs, a shift to solutions away from traditional funds. Alternative UCITS, the European equivalent to the US 40 Act liquid alternative funds, grew by more than 30% a year from 2008 onwards and the exceptional growth of recent years is continuing, with assets growing by a further 34% in the year to March 2015 according to HFMweek UCITS Report 2015. PWC Alternative Asset Management 2020. Lipper Fund Flows reported that Alternative Ucits funds are becoming increasingly popular among European investors and the best-selling asset class attracting inflows of €3.4 billion.

Those with established franchises and long track records are reaping the benefit and in some cases hitting capacity limits, other firms are quickly resourcing people and developing 'me too' products to vie for the growing demand. A report by research firm Spence Johnson showed that the UK market grew by £16.2bn (€22.4bn) over 2014, reaching a total of £124bn. However, by 2019, it predicts the market will be worth £218bn as defined contribution (DC) schemes grow and allocate more.

With proliferation comes the prospect for a wider variance of outcomes, and so it has come to pass. However I can tell you that the marketing material all tends to read similarly, plausibly and credible. This then poses a risk to investors and very real challenge for professional fund buyers. Especially as more investors are buying DGFs as off the shelf single solutions as multi-manager and advised building block approaches are running off. DGFs have also been a lifeline to asset firms because they are a) more resistant to price compression and b) infinitely scalable to the point they become super-feeder funds for entire groups like SLI and Aviva.

**Hitting a Speed-bump:** The surge in flows now coincides with a tough time for the sector in terms of volatility and perhaps underlines the lag between performance and marketing. If we look at SLI GARS as a proxy for other DGFs and one that many seek to emulate then we can see how the fund's volatility has risen steadily in the last year in response to markets.

## Observations:

According to FE Analytics as at 12 February 2015, the difference between the best (CF Odey) and worst performing fund (Woodhill) in the IA Targeted Return sector (now made up of 63 funds) over 1 year was a staggering 37%!

In volatility terms again the differences were stark between the metronomic Sonja Uys' Absolute Insight and Natixis H2O Multi returns, which had 1 year volatility 15 times greater than Absolute Insight. Despite these differences most of these funds are marketed to investors in a similar way. Until recently the vast majority of funds (the median) had been running equity exposure (beta) of around 50% of the total risk allocation. Following 20% losses across many equity markets, many DGF managers, if FE's data is to be believed, have quickly moved to cash (denoted below in light blue), this itself is a bear signal for the broader market. This marries to anecdotal evidence and what I'm hearing on the ground from DGF managers.

> "In a survey of the 35 DGFs which each had at least £30 million of assets -- the minimum size of fund regarded as "investable" for pension funds -- Cambridge Associates found that the median DGF manager lagged a simple 60:40 portfolio by nearly 330 basis points -- 3.3 percentage points -- between 31 October 2007 and 31 March 2015. That equates to £37 for every £100 invested at the beginning of this 7.5 year period." Cambridge Associates Oct15.

**Choosing your SUV:** The danger of buying a DGF is either being seduced by the slick marketing and lifestyle messaging and secondly paying too much. Most DC Consultants snub older legacy 'Managed' funds and yet many operate very similarly to DGF funds albeit within the fairly broad (sensible) confines of the IA/ABI sectors and often at considerable discount to DGFs. They are popularly maligned for being benchmark-driven and yet many are not managed on a relative return basis.

Looking back through the older fund ranges can unearth some relatively inexpensive gems, high are not marketed but can be bought and cannot be closed easily due to vast (largely dormant) pension and insurance assets. Most DGFs I have come across have some central asset allocation (or 'neutral') and few are nearly as unconstrained as they would lead you to believe. That is not to say there isn't some interesting innovation out there (there is) but less of it exists in the mainstream.

If you have decided *unconstrained* is for you, how then best to measure DGF funds? Considerations can include whether: they remain within their stated risk range, deliver meaningful returns through a market cycle, achieve a positive hit rate (more winners than losers) and mitigate losses during market downturns. Thus aggregating the performance of DGFs during periods of stress can be as, or more, telling that their ability to capture rising markets. You need both of course to achieve that elusive asymmetry. On those grounds the general equity sell-off since last summer, oil collapse, gold spike and recent markets have been a test for these funds, many have experienced 6% 6 month drawdowns more than the expected volatility implied.

Indeed recent drawdowns are around 50-60% what we saw during the worst of 2007-2008. One reason (and for me problem) for this is that the majority of strategies are built on a similar premise, to aim for equity like returns over 3-5 years, deliver half the volatility of equities, adopt an 'absolute return' approach with a cash based benchmark through using an unconstrained basket of equity and equity-substitute assets to delver equity-like returns, yet with the loose promise (not guarantee) of lower volatility.

## The Hit Rate (Win/Loss Ratio):

DGF funds can come with a bewildering set of optional extras ('fully loaded') and understanding the drivers of return can take some time. The Hit Rate or 'Win-Loss' ratio is an oft overlooked measure of how complex strategies are delivering across their portfolio. In a pseudo gambling perspective, if a DGF is a book of market bets: does the manager get more bets than wrong? If the answer is less then an outperforming manager has to allocate more risk (bigger bet) to certain trades (like equities). Alternatively if the manager is able to minimise the magnitude of losers relative to gains when in profit: we call this asymmetry or generating positive skew without reversion. With multiple long, short, relative value and cross-trades, all with different investment horizons, then it is sometimes difficult to see the wood for the trees. The Hit Rate captures which strategies are in profit (or loss) since inception or over a time period. It is also a way to quantify the real diversification effect of the portfolio which can sometimes become skewed (misleading) in the traditional gross to net volatility approach. For example when markets stress or correlate, the diversification effect within DGFs can drop rapidly. Since most DGF managers avoid trying to hold costly insurance type assets (Credit Default Swaps, Options) then periods of stress can catch out some managers who find themselves overly exposed to market beta (equities, equity futures, lower grade credit, REITs etc).

The Hit Rate can be viewed alongside upside/downside capture rate, negative month rate and downside related measures like Sortino and Omega. Grinold and Kahn also expressed the relationship between manager skill, IR and number of bets by the approximation: **IR = IC * SQRT(Breadth)**.

Information Ratio equals: Information Coefficient (IC) times the square root of the number of independent bets ('breadth'). This paper discusses the benefits of the Hit Rate for hedge funds: http://www.northinfo.com/documents/238.pdf

**Conclusions:**

The notion of fund buyers trying to CAPm optimise ostensibly similar DGFs together makes me shudder. The only sensible way is to allocate by looking at the different factor exposures fund-to-fund. What factor analysis will tell you is just how similar many of these funds are the same, especially once you ring fence what are ostensibly equity long-short funds first. What you end up with are funds that have a slug of equity exposure, some infrastructure closed-ended funds, some debt yielding positions, some passives, REITs, property, other absolute return funds and a chunk of hedging assets and derivatives. You might get the odd catastrophe bond or esoteric debt fund but their meaningful notional effects are small unless they blow up. You are then left to either buy on the skill, risk management or cost. That shouldn't be surprising, automakers copy each other, some have strategic deals with common platforms like Nissan and Renault, and again similarly we have seen DGF architects move firm to firm. Euan Munro, David Millar, Batty and Jubb, Johanna Kryklund, Michael Spinks. Instead what I look for personally are managers with different philosophies, approaches and portfolio constructions like but not confined to: inflation-based strategies (like Hermes Multi Asset Inflation), lower equity approaches (Church House Tenax and Absolute Insight) or balancing strategies like Nordea's Stable Return and Diversified Return funds. I have paused momentarily on related Income funds, as I'm still trying to assess the chase for yield as to impact on risk budget (Equities, Credit, REITs).

In terms of meeting stated goals, markets (including Brexit) have been a proverbial speed-bump for DGF funds but for now the hubris will continue so long as the flows keep coming in.

The pipeline of new funds continues to swell and the sector will invariably mature as buyers work out the losers and survivors. Whatever you do, buy with the speed bumps in mind, look at the drawdowns, hit ratio, spot the similarities, look for diversifying approaches and kneel down and have a look at how robust the chassis is to handle both smooth and rough roads ahead.

## Life-Support? Guided Funds and Distributors:

In contrast to rating agencies and innovative fintechs that typically have good transparency in terms of business model and methodology; life platforms, distributors and insurers on the other hand actually say very little about their fund governance, manager selection and methodology. What is said is usually vacuous and ambiguous. Much will have been agreed at group level and relates as much to the margin and rebate on offer from fund houses than the merits of underlying funds. Open architecture platforms and supermarkets need only ensure funds are regulated. I refer to platforms that infer a degree of governance and skill in their literature.

What then is available in terms of information is ostensibly marketing rhetoric by and large. Many insurers have supposed 'guided architecture' yet the rationale and reason as to fund changes is far from clear and many ranges appear stagnant and poorly attended.

There are exceptions of course, some platforms publish the minutes of their investment committee, some use agencies and we are seeing more independent governance committees cropping-up (albeit a vast cast of seniors sitting around a table does not in itself guarantee good fund outcomes). Big distributors focus on fairly blunt median outcomes and glacially slow to respond to changes.

What is not talked about publicly is the out-dated IT Infrastructures within many insurers today, a legacy of early pre-Cloud computerisation attempts from the 1970s until the millennia. The result is a huge legacy of funds relating to now defunct products and a huge number of funds actually on platforms are soft-closed. Reality bites in as much few distributors find it easy to close old products fully, many of the original system knowledge lost. Therefore what a customer sees is an integration of the truth but it also means insurers and platforms are burdened to monitor old funds alongside new. In short advisers and customers should complete due diligence on insurers, wealth platforms and guided buy lists exactly in the same way as for rating agencies. The challenge for platforms and insurers is to become more attentive and transparent around the funds added and removed to a platform or to outsource.

These facts have been long known in the industry but most commission-led advisers were reasonably happy to ignore or had long moved away from building block funds to passives or newer risk-guided 'solutions'. The advent of RDR changes the game. Fund buyers would do well to understand the limitations of the behemoth providers and validate that any marketing claims are fair, clear and not misleading. Transparency is upon us.

**Solution - Rating the Raters: due diligence!** If some but not all agencies have merit then buyers need to conduct their own due diligence when choosing. Firstly, understand the business model belying the rating. Does the agency employ the pay to play model, marketing fees or subscription service? What size is the recommended list, is it quant, qual, does it rely on humint or digital models, how many analysts are there relative to fund coverage, what period have they covered the fund, their relevant experience of the manager/sector, the frequency of reviews, rating turnover, rating format: face to face, by phone or questionnaire? If you don't know the answers then how can you interpret the quality of a recommended fund belying the rating?

Secondly buyers should feel confident to challenge an agency on any rating or unexpected outcome. Persistency is a moot point, few agencies I know chart the risk adjusted outcomes of the funds they rate over time. They should! Also in a post Dodd-Frank sense, agencies should have advisory boards and non executives to provide independent challenge.

**Future State - Crowd Ratings?** Most fund buyers over-estimate their relationships with fund managers, something I explored in *'Key Man Misnomer'*. To most fund managers, fund analysts are a necessary inconvenience and more agencies = overload. Consequently fund managers will not tell analysts everything and, by law, physical torture isn't allowed (no telephone directories or hammer was used your honour!). Few agencies interview ancillary staff, which is a mistake in my view. Comparing notes between investment office and fund manager can be enlightening.

Therefore human intelligence has a place but can always fail (on occasion) and needs to be far more forensic and varied than has traditionally been the case. Like fund managers, I advocate local boutique agencies over global conglomerates and single out the good efforts of FundCalibre, Fund House, SharingAlpha, Square Mile and Pure Group to name a few.

My hope is that in time common standards can be agreed and that agencies can network to improve the quality of fund intelligence. This jars somewhat with my issue of ratings overlap, admittedly. Here I am looking for synergy not group think. Complimentary rather than mere duplication. Curiously the FMYA judging panel, effectively, is a crowd sourced approach and an enjoyable experience at that. It avoids game theory 'safe options'. Just like diversifying assets, fund managers or platforms, diversifying analysts (whom deliver different perspectives) will add value.

**Creating the New Fund Order?** I hope you have enjoyed this latest installment of the suitcase fund analyst. With version 2.0 my intention was always to provide some solutions to fund selectors, fintechs and fund managers alike. I hope I have come closer to that. Since first writing NFO1.0 I have begun to get more actively involved with fintechs and the industry at large in advisory, ambassador and media capacities, building my own knowledge. Key personal projects being; firstly a new AMC model that compensates (passes-on) economies of scale back to the end investor, as the fund grows in size. Secondly the incentives of fund managers and how they are remunerated and aligned to the end customer. A new form of 'Long-Term Investment Plan' is overdue. Thirdly, transparency of charges is again critical to rebuilding trust and last (but not least) a digitalised global due diligence template via the APFI.

My friend, and fellow writer, Tom Chatfielfd was keen to note (during our interview at a Berlin conference) that NFO.1.0 asked a question, as to a 'digital death', rather than made a post-mortem statement. He is right of course, it is a question and it will be answered either by apathy or action. Similarly my friend (and fellow APFI director) and luminary Roland Meerdter will argue that digitalisation does not necessarily itself mean obsoletion. He points to a 'third way', to become cyborgs, symbiotic with machines.

I share this hope but as Martin Ford (author of the Rise of the Robots) wrote:

**"the ongoing race between technology and education may well be approaching the endgame: the machines are coming for the higher skill jobs as well." P.124 'White Jobs at Risk' Chapter 4, Oneworld, 2015.**

Whatever the outcome I firmly remain a fund buyer for both my current insurer and boutique platform Gemini. My work for the APFI and CISI also continues where I can influence best practice. Likewise I am able to have a voice through various think tanks. I hope to consult into the fund strategy of asset managers and fintechs alike, and begin to shape what the new fund order may come to look like. If you want to talk then I am only a suitcase away.

Time to pack the Peli once more.. Fides est Fortis!

#newfundorder

*'I'm used to dealing with the dead. The only emotion I feel about one of these is a faint hope it may be a Party official'.*
IMDB, From the Film Gorky Park (1983).


## ABOUT THE AUTHOR: Jon 'JB' Beckett, Chartered MCSI

Self-dubbed blue collar CIO. Once amateur painter, a lover of classic cars and car chase films. Affectionately (or infamously) known, JB has long been an outsider of the 'City', a Scot looking in, challenging the status quo and casting light on the, at times, incestuous relationship between fund selectors and fund managers. JB has been a fund selector/strategist with over 20 years industry experience. Having initially worked in IFA compliance; JB's fund selector career started as a para planner and non-discretionary portfolio manager, for a small/medium-sized IFA, at the turn of the millennium. There he created asset allocation models, managed a 200-fund buy list, building risk-rated portfolios for mass affluent clients. Later he moved to fund analysis and product management for Franklin Templeton in 2003. Redundancy, post credit crisis, saw JB move through group insight and complex product governance roles, before returning as a fund selector and gatekeeper for a £100bn-plus UK retail and institutional proposition. Subsequently, JB is consulting Chief Investment Officer to the Gemini Investment Management Ltd board, UK Research Lead for the Association of Professional Fund Investors (profundinvestors.com), Ambassador for the Transparency Task Force, Chartered Member, Author and Senior Reviewer with the Chartered Institute for Securities and Investments (CISI.org) and member of the Z/Yen (zen.com) Long Finance think-tank.

Throughout JB has been a boutique fund advocate, a 'turbulent priest', a leading voice on fund governance and transparency, and a controversial media personality in the fund world (and not only because of his extensive tattoos).

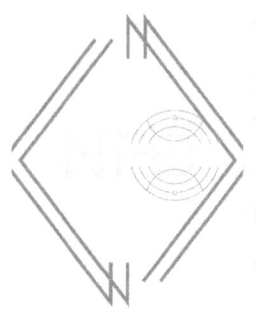

## Acknowledgements

Graham Russel (Proof Reader v.1.0)

*My warm gratitude to the following:*
My wife Jenny Beckett
My father Syd Beckett, mother Margaret Beckett
Andrew Parry
Bull Bulloch
Chris Arnott, Standard Life Investments
Chris Williams, WealthHorizon
Dr Brian Fleming, Standard Life Investments
Dr John Marke
Dr Michael Mainelli. Z/Yen
Ezekiel Cheever
Lawrence Gosling, Incisive Media
Harry Dickinson, Harrington Cooper
James Phillips, Citywire
Jesus Soborol, Citywire
Mahyad Gilani
Oren Kaplan, SharingAlpha.com
Patrick Murphy, Pure Group
Robin Powell, journalist and presenter
Rory Maguire, Fundhouse
Shiv Taneja

Sir John Templeton

Stuart Alexander

Tesla Motor Cars

Tom Chatfield, digital activist

*I acknowledge the following in making this book:*

Aberdeen Asset Management

'Active Share' studies by Patijisto and Cremmer (2009)

AdviceOS

AdvisorShares

Apple Corp.

Arch Cru

Artemis

Association of Professional Fund Investors

Barclays Wealth

Bernard Beckett, writer

BNY Mellon

British Broadcasting Corporation

BSkyB

BT Sport

Cambridge Associates

Capita

CASS Business School

Caterham F1

Cazenove

Chartered Institute for Securities and Investments

Citywire publishing

Credit Suisse

Daimler Benz

English Premiership

European Securities and Markets Authority

Fidelity Investment Limited

Finametrica

FirstTrust

Football Association

Franklin Templeton Investments

Freakonomics and Superfreakonomics, by Steven Levitt and Stephen Dubner

FT Adviser

Fund Forum, ICBI

Gemini Investment Management

Godzilla (film 1954)

Goldman Sachs

Google Money

Grosvenor House Hotel

GURU

HVPW

IndexIQ

The Investment Association

Invesco Perpetual

Investec

IShares

John Bogle

John Chatfield-Roberts

JP Morgan

Julex

LinkedIn

London Transport

Martin Ford 'The Rise of the Robots' 2015, Oneworld

M&G

Makers and writers of Gorky Park and Three Days of the Condor

Mosaic magazine

NESA

New City Initiative

http://www.northinfo.com/documents/238.pdf

Nutmeg

Powershares

Proshares

QuantShares

Samuel Beckett, writer, poet and playwright

Schroders

Scottish Widows

SensibleInvesting.tv

ShareAction

SPDR

Square Mile Investment & Research Consulting

Standard & Poor's

Standard Life

Strategic Insight

Sun Tzu

Sydney Pollack

The Royal Albert Hall

Thistle Barbican
Tom Clancy
True and Fair Campaign
Twitter
United States Department of Defense
Vanguard

*Attributed:*

Bernie Madoff (United States v Bernard L. Madoff) 09 CR 213 (DC)
JP Morgan

*I refer to the following sources:*

BA Business Life magazine
Common Sense of Mutual Funds by John Bogle, 1999, John Wiley & Sons
Competition Markets Authority
'Complex Adaptive Systems & Resilience' by Dr John Marke, 2009
Crowdsourcing.org
Financial Conduct Authority
Fundology by John Chatfield-Roberts, 2006, Harriman House
Harrington Cooper wealth manager study
HFMweek UCITS Report 2015
IGS Global Insight
InformationWeek.com.
Analytics. 'Accelerating Wall Street 2010. Next Stop: Nanoseconds' by Daniel Safarik, June 2010
investopedia.com
Institutional Pensions Europe

Journal of Finance 'Mutual Fund Performance and the Incentive to Generate Alpha' by Diane Del Guercio and Jonathan Reuter http://onlinelibrary.wiley.com/doi/10.1111/jofi.12048/abstract

Larch Lane *'Hedge Fund Seeding: A Compelling Alternative'.*

Lipper FundFlash, Lipper (a Thomson Reuters company)

Local Government Pension Scheme report, Hymans Robertson

Markus Hill wrote *'Real Assets and Funds Boutiques – Seed Money and German "Middle Class Thinking"'* in 2011.

*New City Initiative and Open Europe published a paper in June 2015 entitled 'Asset management in Europe: The case for reform'*

Parkinson's Law: The Pursuit of Progress, by C. Northcote Parkinson, 1958, John Murray

PWC Alternative Asset Management 2020

Real-World Economics Review, issue no. 50 'What is Minsky all about, anyway?' By KorkutErtürk and GökcerÖzgür [University of Utah, USA]

Schroders Q3 2013 earnings update

Sheffield Hawarth

Ship Traffic Control: Controlling Ships in Heavy Traffic' in Mosaic January 1975

Sportingintelligence Global Sports Survey, reprinted in BA Business Life 11.2013

Supership' by Noel Mostert, October 1974

Stephen G. Meyer, Executive Vice President of SEI

The Black Swan by Nassim Nicholas Taleb, 2007, Random House

Wikimedia Commons

wikipedia.com

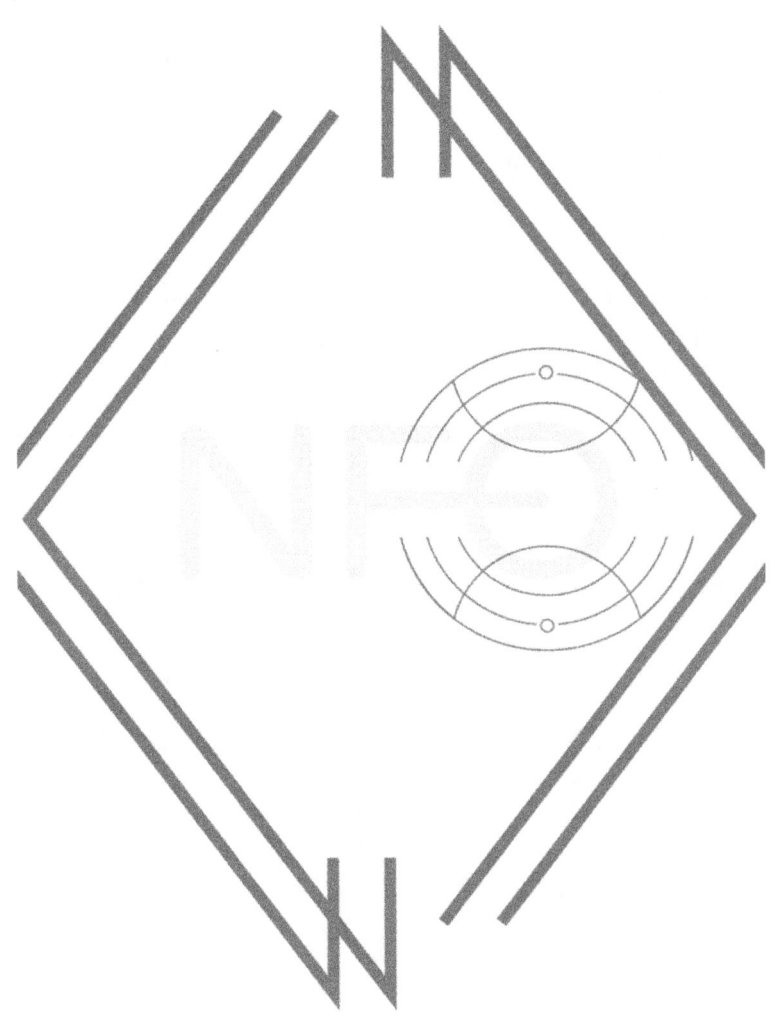

www.ingramcontent.com/pod-product-compliance
Lightning Source LLC
Chambersburg PA
CBHW060828170526
45158CB00001B/116